Becoming A Writer

Becoming A Writer

Developing Academic Writing Skills

Rita Wong • Eric Glendinning
Helen Mantell

Longman

BECOMING A WRITER: DEVELOPING ACADEMIC WRITING SKILLS

Adaptation of Write Ideas: An Intermediate Course in Writing Skills, by Eric Glendinning and Helen Mantell. Published by Longman Group Limited, 1983.

Longman, 10 Bank Street, White Plains, N.Y. 10606

Associate companies:
Longman Group Ltd., London
Longman Cheshire Pty., Melbourne
Longman Paul Pty., Auckland
Copp Clark Pitman, Toronto
Pitman Publishing Inc., New York

Distributed in the United Kingdom by Longman Group Ltd., Longman House,
Burnt Hill, Harlow, Essex CM20 2JE, England, and by associated
companies, branches, and representatives throughout the world.

Executive editor: Joanne Dresner
Project editor: Penny Laporte
Text design: Joseph DePinho
Text art and photo credits: See page 82
Production supervisor: Eduardo Castillo

Library of Congress Cataloging in Publication Data

Wong, Rita.
  Becoming a writer.

  Adaptation of: Write ideas—An intermediate course
in writing skills/by Eric Glendinning
and Helen Mantell. 1983.
  1. English language—Rhetoric. 2. Report writing.
3. English language—Textbooks for foreign speakers.
I. Glendinning, Eric. II. Mantell, Helen.
III. Glendinning, Eric. Write ideas. IV. Title.
PE1478.W66 1987   808'.042   87–16935
ISBN 0–582–90722–5

6 7 8 9 10-KE-959493

Contents

Introduction

Becoming a Writer is designed to lead intermediate-level students of English from the generation of ideas to the expression of those ideas in writing. It is intended for upper secondary school students and adult learners with academic or professional goals.

AIMS AND PRINCIPLES

Many students find writing the most difficult skill to acquire. Even if they can meet the writing demands made in their English course, they find difficulty in handling the writing required for study or work. **Becoming a Writer** was written to help students cope with the writing demands made in typical study and work situations.

Good writing involves not only the accurate use of language, but also the effective organization of information. In addition, it requires the writer to be aware of the reader's needs, both when selecting content and guiding the reader through the writing. Another important skill is selecting relevant data to support an argument or explanation. The skills of selecting relevant information, organizing it effectively, expressing it in accurate language and guiding the reader through the finished piece of writing are the skills dealt with in this book.

The writing session should not be a totally silent time, with work submitted at the end to the teacher, the sole reader for most student writing. **Becoming a Writer** encourages the student to think of the reader while writing. In many cases, the work will be read and commented on by fellow students. Students must be given time to think ideas out for themselves and discipline their thoughts on paper; but the exchange of ideas before and comparison of results after writing are an extremely valuable part of the lesson and should not be omitted.

ORGANIZATION

Each of the eight chapters begins with a section called *Getting Started*, which introduces the learners to the unit by engaging them in a preliminary task. Most require a brief period of individual work, then a comparison in pairs, followed by a class discussion. This task is designed to promote discussion of the main points covered in the unit. Using this exercise as a stimulus for thought, students should be able to discover for themselves the basis for the organizational points covered in the unit.

The main points of each unit are illustrated through a combination of *tasks* and guiding comments. Shaded boxes throughout the unit help to encapsulize the main points.

The *Summary Task* at the end of each unit ties the points of the unit together and focuses on the cumulative knowledge gained up to that unit of the book. This final task provides a choice of exercises for students to complete on their own. The topics are drawn from a range of subject areas (some already discussed in the unit, some discussed in previous units, some chosen according to the individual student's interests). These exercises call for an interest in the subject rather than a specialized knowledge of it. Instructions for this task include a summary of the organizational and language points treated in the unit, to help students organize their final piece of writing.

The *Reference Section* in the back of the book is an integral part of the text. It contains examples of completed tasks against which students can compare their work, additional explanations and practice exercises, and answers to selected tasks. Students are referred to the reference section at various points in the book.

THE TASKS

Two types of tasks are provided in the text. The first type focuses on giving learners experience with some of the processes involved in written expression. These tasks require learners to consider the reader both in selecting content and in guiding the reader through the writing. Learners read and comment on their fellow writers' work as a part of this process. They also learn to revise their writing on the basis of readers' comments.

The second type of task focuses on language forms that support the expression of ideas at the discourse level, for example: the use of relative clauses in expressing degrees of importance; grammatical forms that link one sentence to another; forms of paragraph structure; and typical language used to write descriptions, comparisons, explanations, arguments, and problems and solutions.

It is hoped that with this book students will better understand the process of becoming a writer.

Acknowledgments

I would like to thank Eric Glendinning and Helen Mantell for creating **Write Ideas**, the parent of **Becoming a Writer**, for without the parent, there would be no child. I would also like to express my appreciation to Joanne Dresner and Penny Laporte, talented colleagues whose insight and editorial savvy underlie both the process of completing this project and the product itself.

1 Preparing to Write

GETTING STARTED

You are going to write a description of a class member for your class newspaper. But first, let's try to prepare for this description.

◆ With a partner, look at a reporter's notes from an interview of Bruce Springsteen. Use this information to write a description of the rock star. When you have finished, compare your description with one written by another student. Then read the description in the reference section on page 71.

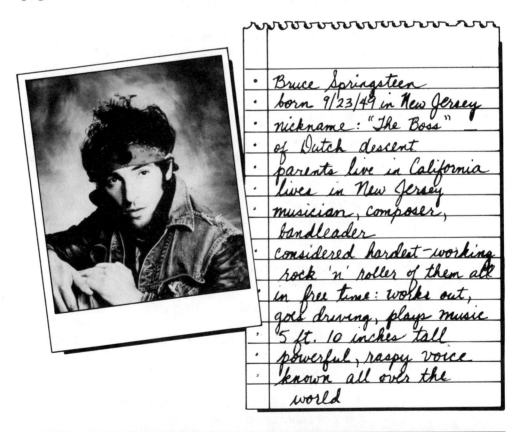

- Bruce Springsteen
- born 9/23/49 in New Jersey
- nickname: "The Boss"
- of Dutch descent
- parents live in California
- lives in New Jersey
- musician, composer, bandleader
- considered hardest-working rock 'n' roller of them all
- in free time: works out, goes driving, plays music
- 5 ft. 10 inches tall
- powerful, raspy voice
- known all over the world

As you have just seen, writing the description of Bruce Springsteen involved organizing information and putting it together so that the reader can see which piece of information is more important than another. In this chapter, you will begin to learn how to organize information.

LISTING AND SELECTING

> One way to begin writing is to make a list of as many points about a topic as you can.

◆ **TASK 1.**   Let's say you have been asked to give a presentation on your hometown to people who have never been there. What would you tell them? What would you choose to describe? Its geography? Its history?

A. Make a list of points you could include. Compare your list with another class member's. Discuss any differences.

B. Now look at page 72 for a list of possible points. How many do you have on your list? Were there some on your list that were not on this one?

◆ **TASK 2.**   Now that you have made a list of possible points for the presentation on your hometown, you must select the most appropriate ones for your audience.

A. Look at your list. Which points would you include in your talk for each of the following groups?

1. Tourists, with a particular interest in history, planning a weekend visit
2. Business people, some who have young families, planning to move to your city to work
3. Students coming to study in your city for two years

B. Compare and discuss your choices with a class member. Did your choices differ depending on your audience?

◆ **TASK 3.**   The following is a question from an examination.

> What is a good language learner?

A. Decide which of the points listed below you would choose to discuss in your answer. Select the ones that are most directly related to the question.

1. motivation
2. sex
3. age
4. personality
5. native language

6. educational background
7. appearance
8. intelligence
9. occupation
10. family

B. Compare your list with that of another student. Discuss your choices.

◆ **TASK 4.**   A class of future teachers was asked this question.

What is a good teacher?

How would you answer this question? List your points and then compare them with those of another student. Select the most relevant points from each of your lists and discuss them with the rest of the class.

ORGANIZING

> In preparing to write, you began by listing possible points and then selecting the most suitable ones for the topic and for the audience. The next step is to organize these points to help the reader follow them more easily.

Grouping Information

One way of organizing is to group information into categories of similar items or ideas.

◆ **TASK 5.**   If you were preparing an exhibit on the *History of Flying* for a museum, how would you organize the topics pictured below? Compare your order with that of another student.

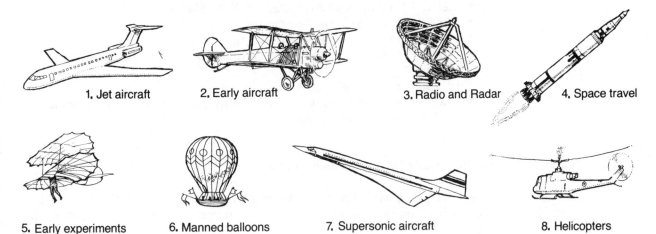

1. Jet aircraft   2. Early aircraft   3. Radio and Radar   4. Space travel

5. Early experiments   6. Manned balloons   7. Supersonic aircraft   8. Helicopters

◆ **TASK 6.** Look at these points from a student's essay on her country. Organize the points by putting similar points together into one group and decide on a heading for each group. For example, *mountains* and *rivers and lakes* could be in a group with the heading *geography*. Compare your organization with that of another student.

1. industry
2. folk dances
3. examinations
4. winter sports
5. agriculture
6. typical foods
7. mountains
8. presidency
9. main regions
10. football teams
11. rivers and lakes
12. political parties
13. universities
14. national dress
15. exports
16. festivals

Expressing Degrees of Importance

In addition to grouping information, you can organize information by identifying which information is more important and which is less important.

◆ **TASK 7.** Look at the following information about the inventor of the ball point pen, Ladislao Biro, who died in 1985. Imagine that it is 1985; you are a newspaper reporter, and Mr. Biro has just died. You have been given the assignment of writing an obituary of Mr. Biro for a local newspaper.

In preparation, arrange the sentences so that related ideas are together. Then, decide which information is more important and which information is less important. Mark the important information with a + and the less important information with a −. Compare your results with those of another student.

Ladislao Biro
- born in Hungary in 1899
- emigrated to Argentina in 1940
- invented the ball point pen in 1942
- sold his design of a hand-operated clothes washer at the age of 17
- met the President of Argentina in Yugoslavia
- went to Yugoslavia on vacation
- invented more than 30 successful inventions
- the ball point pen is the most common ink-writing device in the world
- invented heat-proof tile
- the President of Argentina invited Biro to emigrate to Argentina
- died in Argentina in 1985

Identifying Main and Subordinate Clauses

Now that you have identified the relative importance of the information about Biro, you need to rewrite the information for the reader. Look at this sentence.

> Ladislao Biro, who died yesterday in Argentina, was the inventor of the ball point pen.

Which is more important, the fact that he died or the fact that he was the inventor of the ball point pen? In this sentence, the fact that he was the inventor of the ball point pen is more important because this information is given in the main clause. The information about his death is given in the subordinate clause, and so it has less importance.

> Main clause: *Ladislao Biro was the inventor of the ball point pen.*
> Subordinate clause: *who died yesterday in Argentina*

How can you tell which clause is the main clause and which is the subordinate clause? All clauses have a subject and a verb, but subordinate clauses begin with a subordinating word. In this example, the word is *who*.

Identifying Relative Clauses

Clauses that begin with *who, which,* or *that* are called relative clauses. Look at these examples.

> 1. The president of Argentina, *who met Biro in Yugoslavia,* invited the inventor to emigrate to Argentina.
> 2. The ball point pen, *which was invented by Biro,* is the most common ink-writing device in the world.
> 3. The invention *that made Biro famous* is the ball point pen.

Notice the comma before *who* and the comma after *Yugoslavia* in the first sentence. If we took out the clause between the commas, we would have the main clause *The president of Argentina invited the inventor to emigrate to Argentina.* When relative clauses are enclosed by commas, it means that the information in these clauses is simply descriptive. Relative clauses are useful ways to add descriptive information to your writing.

By comparison, notice that in the last sentence, no commas precede or follow the relative clause *that made Biro famous.* This type of relative clause is not simply descriptive. It defines the noun, in this case, *invention.*

When are *who, which* and *that* used. Can you explain the rules for the use of these pronouns? Write the rules here.

_____

_____

_____

_____

You can also use *where* to describe or identify places, as in the following examples.

> 1. Biro emigrated to Argentina, *where he lived until his death.*
> 2. The country *where Biro lived for half of his life* is Argentina.

Whose is used to show possession, as in the following example.

> Ladislao Biro, *whose ball point pen is used throughout the world,* died in Argentina in 1985.

◆ **TASK 8.**   Practice identifying and writing main and subordinate clauses.

A. Look at the edited description of Bruce Springsteen on page 71 in the reference section. Find the three subordinate relative clauses and write them below.

_____

_____

_____

_____

_____

B. In the following sentence, change the meaning of the sentence by making the fact that Biro died more important than the fact that he had invented the ball point pen.

> Ladislao Biro, who died yesterday in Argentina, was the inventor of the ball point pen.

_____

C. Combine these two ideas into one sentence. Make the first idea more important than the second. Then rewrite the sentence and make the second idea more important than the first.

- Biro was born in Hungary in 1899.
- He emigrated to Argentina in 1940.

_____

_____

Turn to page 72 in the reference section if you feel you need additional practice with relative clauses.

◆ **TASK 9.** You should now be ready to write your obituary of Ladislao Biro. When you have completed your obituary, compare it with that of another student. Did you agree on which information was more important and which was less important?

SUMMARY TASK

◆ Interview someone in your class. Find out as much as you can. Look at the information you have and select what you think other members of the class would be interested in knowing. After you have selected this information, decide which is the most important. Show which information is more important and which is less important by putting the important information in main clauses and the less important information in subordinate clauses. After you have written your first copy, show it to someone else in your class. Ask that person to read it and give you any suggestions to help make it clearer. Make any changes you need to and then prepare your final version.

Preparing several versions of a piece of writing is a natural process for writers. Each version before the final one is called a *draft*. Getting suggestions from other writers is also a helpful part of the process. Talking about your writing with someone else helps you clarify your own thoughts. Throughout this book, you will have many opportunities to experience this process of becoming a writer.

Connecting and Arranging Ideas

GETTING STARTED

◆ The sentences in the following paragraph are out of order. Can you put them in their original order?

1. It was founded by Sandra Felton, a high school mathematics teacher, who got tired of finding socks in the living room and shoes in the kitchen.
2. They can also attend an annual seminar.
3. Many of the members of Messies Anonymous are women with jobs outside the home.
4. Messies Anonymous is an organization that tries to help messy people change their ways.
5. These women get help from the organization's quarterly newsletter and can buy Messies Manual, a 157-page book written by Mrs. Felton.

Compare your arrangement with another student's. Discuss the reasons for your order.

> In writing, ideas are connected and arranged in the form of paragraphs. A well-formed paragraph has a structure. As a result, even though the sentences in such a paragraph have been mixed up, the paragraph can be reassembled into its original form. In this chapter, you are going to examine structures of paragraphs and practice building them.

EXAMINING PARAGRAPH STRUCTURES

How did you decide which of the sentences on Messies Anonymous came first? If you looked for the most general statement, you used a good strategy.

The Foundation

> The most general statement serves as a foundation for the rest of the sentences. This statement is like the trunk of a tree, and the rest of the sentences are like the branches of the tree.

◆ **TASK 1.** Circle the most general statement in each group of sentences below.

1. a. Many people are afraid of going to the dentist.
   b. They associate the experience with pain.
   c. In fact, modern dentistry has made dental work virtually painless.

2. a. As each tooth comes out, children place the tooth under their pillow before they go to sleep.
   b. They expect the tooth fairy to come while they are sleeping and exchange the tooth for a small sum of money.
   c. In American folklore, the loss of one's first teeth is associated with a set of common practices.

3. a. A club is used to hit a ball around a course.
   b. In Scotland, it does not cost a great deal of money to play this sport, but in Japan, only the rich can afford to.
   c. Golf is a popular international sport which was invented in Scotland.
4. a. The capital of the 50th state of the U.S. is on the island of Oahu.
   b. Hawaii consists of 8 islands located about 2,000 miles southwest of San Francisco.
   c. The largest island is also called Hawaii.
5. a. Nearly 60 different materials are used in a car's construction.
   b. The average car is assembled from 15,000 parts.
   c. The modern car is a complex machine.

The Branches

If we think of the foundation sentence as the trunk of a tree, the other sentences are like the branches of a tree. Consider what a tree of the paragraph on Messies Anonymous would look like. The numbers on the tree refer to the numbers identifying the statements at the beginning of this chapter, on page **8**.

As you can see, these branching statements follow a specific order. If the most general statement is the first sentence in the paragraph, how are the remaining sentences ordered? Let's look more closely at this paragraph.

Messies Anonymous is an organization that tries to help messy people change their ways. *It* was founded by Sandra Felton, a high school mathematics teacher, who got tired of finding socks in the living room and shoes in the kitchen. Many of the *members of Messies Anonymous* are women with jobs outside the home. *These women* can get help from the organization's quarterly newsletter, and can buy <u>Messies</u> <u>Manual</u>, a 157-page book written by Mrs. Felton. *They* can *also* attend the annual seminar.

What clues help establish this order?

- Sentence 4 introduces the organization of Messies Anonymous to the reader and is therefore the opening statement.

- Two clues suggest that sentence 1 follows next. First, the pronoun *it* tells the reader to look for the noun *it* refers to. In this case, the noun is Messies Anonymous. Sentence 1 also gives historical information about the organization. This kind of information is likely to follow the general statement in a paragraph. To show the connection between these two sentences, an arrow has been drawn from *it* to *Messies Anonymous*. Drawing arrows can help show the links between sentences.
- Sentence 3 comes next. It gives further information about Messies Anonymous, specifically about the members. Again, an arrow has been drawn to show the connection between *Messies Anonymous* and *members of Messies Anonymous*.
- *These women* in sentence 5 refers the reader back to *women* mentioned earlier. Draw an arrow to connect these words.
- The final statement, sentence 2, is linked to the rest of the paragraph in two ways. The pronoun *they* points the reader back to a plural noun in the preceding sentence—in this case, *women*. The word *also* tells the reader that there was an earlier, related event—in this case, *can get help* and *can buy*. Draw arrows to show these links.

Grammar Links in a Paragraph

A well-written, cohesive paragraph links sentences together.

The arrows above showed you how the connections were made between sentences in the paragraph on Messies Anonymous. Let's look more closely at the ways in which the sentences in paragraphs are connected, beginning with grammar links.

Nouns and Pronouns

In the paragraph on Messies Anonymous you saw how pronouns refer back to nouns already mentioned and, therefore, form a link between the sentences in which they appear.

◆ **TASK 2.** Show how pronouns and nouns form links between sentences. Draw a line between the italicized pronouns and the nouns or noun phrases they refer to. The first one is done for you.

Many working women have had trouble keeping their households neat and clean. No one did anything about *it*, however, until Sandra Felton came along. The 50-year-old high school mathematics teacher started a discussion group for messy people. *They* would gather to discuss *their* problems and frustrations. *Their* meetings were the beginning of Messies Anonymous. Mrs. Felton says that although her mother was a "cleanie," she had always been a "messy." However, *she* has finally found a system which has helped her overcome *her* messiness.

Nouns

Sometimes you may not want to use a pronoun because the noun was mentioned many sentences earlier and the reader may not remember what the pronoun is referring to. There are also times when using a pronoun would lead to confusion. The reader may not know which noun to refer back to, as in the following example.

> Mrs. Felton says that her mother was a "cleanie." *She* has finally found a system to ovecome *her* messiness.

Does *she* refer to Mrs. Felton or to her mother? Who does *her* refer to? It is unclear. In these cases, there are several other ways of referring to a previously mentioned noun.

- Let us say the noun is *Mrs. Felton.* You can repeat the noun, *Mrs. Felton,* especially if you want to stress the name.
- Some nouns first appear in the plural form, or are preceded by the article *a.* When the noun is repeated, *a* often changes to *the* or *this;* the plural form often adds *the* or *these. The, this* and *these* are the links between sentences. For example: Mrs. Felton formed *a* discussion *group. The group* would gather to talk about messiness.
- You can also use a variation of the noun. In the example above, instead of repeating *discussion group,* you could write *group.* Because the noun has already been introduced, the reader understands which group you are referring to.
- Finally, instead of repeating a noun, a descriptive noun phrase can be used. For example, *Mrs. Felton* could be replaced by *the 50-year-old high school teacher.*

In the next two tasks you will practice recognizing how nouns and pronouns form links to nouns mentioned earlier in a paragraph.

◆ **TASK 3.** Look at the italicized nouns. How are they linked to other sentences in the paragraph? Draw a line to the words linking these sentences and put a circle around these words. The first one is done for you.

Insulin is *a hormone* made by the pancreas. This hormone is used to treat *diabetes,* a disease that involves having too much sugar in the blood. Diabetes can harm almost every organ system: the eyes, the kidneys, the nerves, and the blood vessels. *Diabetics* may suffer a variety of *illnesses.* They are especially subject to heart attacks and strokes, kidney failure, blindness, nerve damage, or impotence. Although *the hormone* was discovered over a half century ago, scientists are just now beginning to understand how it works.

◆ **TASK 4.** Complete the sentences below. Choose appropriate nouns or pronouns to link the second sentence to the first. After you have finished, compare your work with that of another student. The first one is done for you.

1. Bruce Springsteen, considered the hardest rock'n'roller of them all, lives a busy life. When *this hard-working musician* is not performing, _____ works out, goes for a drive, or plays music.

2. Ladislao Biro, who invented the ball point pen, died in 1985. Although the ball point pen was _____ most well-known invention, _____ developed more than 30 successful inventions in his lifetime.

3. The Challenger flight began with excitement and ended with sadness. _____ exploded seconds after _____ took off, killing all seven astronauts aboard.

4. Diabetes can affect almost every organ in the body. Fortunately, _____ can be treated with insulin.

5. Scientists discovered insulin over a half century ago. _____ do not, however, fully understand how _____ works.

Verbs

You have seen in the previous section how one noun is linked to another when it refers to the same person or event.

> Bruce Springsteen, considered the hardest rock'n'roller of them all, lives a busy life. When *this hard-working musician* is not performing, he. . . .

Verbs can also make these links. Look at the following example.

> Earthquakes *occur* somewhere in the world almost every day. Some earthquakes are very slight, but others, like the one which *happened* in Mexico City in 1985, are very severe.

When it is possible, writers try to avoid repeating the same words. They try to find a synonym or an alternative way of expressing the same idea. In the example above, the writer used the verb *occur* in the first sentence and the verb *happened* in the second.

◆ **TASK 5.**   Suggest an alternative verb for the italicized ones below. Write your verb above the original.

1. Messies Anonymous *tries* to help messy people change their ways.

2. Messies Anonymous *was founded* by Sandra Felton.

3. Insulin *is made* by the pancreas.

4. Diabetes *can harm* almost every organ in the body.

5. Diabetics *can get* heart attacks or strokes.

Nouns and Verbs

Another type of linking is one between a noun and a verb, or between two nouns with related forms. Consider the following examples.

> • Sandra Felton started a group to allow messy people *to meet* and to discuss their problems. Their *meetings* were the beginning of Messies Anonymous.
> • Bruce Springsteen is famous for his rock'n'roll *music.* Not only is he an excellent *musician,* he is also a composer and bandleader.

In the first example, the verb phrase *to meet* and the noun *meetings* refer to the same idea. In the second example, *music* and *musician* are related nouns.

◆ **TASK 6.**   Complete the sentences below with an appropriate verb or noun to refer to the italicized word.

1. Biro, the *inventor* of the ball point pen, also created more than 30 other successful _____.

2. The history of *flying* is fascinating, especially when you consider the first _____ and the current _____ into space.

3. Insulin is used to *treat* diabetes. With regular _____, diabetics can lead normal lives.

4. Messies Anonymous was _____ by Sandra Felton. Her *organization* now has 6,000 members.

◆ **TASK 7.** In this exercise you will practice identifying all the grammar links described in this chapter. Draw a line from the italicized word or words to the nouns or verbs they refer to.

A placebo is a type of medicine which is given to benefit or please a patient. *The benefits* are not the result of *its* action as a drug. Instead *they* come from the psychological effect of taking *the drug*. Often *the patient* feels better, but the improvement may last only a short time. Doctors should therefore treat patients with *dummy drugs* only after other *treatment* has failed.

Idea Links in a Paragraph

You have just finished examining some of the grammar links that connect sentences. Idea links are ways of connecting ideas in sentences.

Expressing Reasons and Results

Read the following paragraph.

> Sandra Felton is a high school mathematics teacher who was tired of finding socks in the living room and shoes in the kitchen, *so* she straightened up the house, changed her attitude toward cleaning, and founded Messies Anonymous, an organization that tries to help messy people change their ways. *As a result of* Mrs. Felton's action, more than 6,000 messies are now getting help through her organization.

By using the word *so,* the writer shows the relationship between ideas in the first part of the sentence and ideas in the second. *So* introduces results and reasons. Another phrase that introduces results is *as a result of.* Notice that *so* is followed by a subject and a verb; it connects clauses. *As a result of* is followed by a noun phrase; it connects sentences. A third phrase is simply *as a result.* This phrase introduces a subject and a verb; it also connects sentences. For example:

> A student missed the scholarship application deadline. *As a result,* she could not be considered for that particular scholarship.

◆ **TASK 8.** Complete the following sentences. Use *so, as a result of,* or *as a result.*

1. American children believe in the tooth fairy, _____ they faithfully place the teeth that they lose under their pillows.

2. Many people are afraid of dentists, _____ they avoid going to the dentist.

3. Many people are afraid of dentists. _____, dentists are trying to develop programs to educate people and eliminate their fears.

4. Many people are afraid of dentists. _____ this fear, they do not get the dental care they need.

5. Modern dentistry's improved techniques reduce the pain associated with earlier visits to the dentist. _____, more people will receive better dental care today than in the past.

Expressing Cause and Effect

Look at the following sentences. What is the idea that links these sentences?

> American children faithfully put the teeth they lose under their pillows. They know the tooth fairy will come and exchange their teeth for money.

One common way to connect cause and effect is to use the word *because*. Notice what happens to the form of these two sentences when we link them with *because*.

> American children faithfully put the teeth they lose under their pillows *because* they know the tooth fairy will come and exchange their teeth for money.

Many writers confuse *because* and *because of*. Look at how *because of* is used in the following sentence. Can you explain how *because of* differs from *because*?

> American children faithfully put the teeth they lose under their pillows because of their knowledge that the tooth fairy will come and exchange their teeth for money.

◆ **TASK 9.** Complete the following sentences with either *because* or *because of*.

1. Copper is used for electric wires _____ it conducts well.

2. Copper is used for electric wires _____ its conducting properties.

3. The Golden Gate Bridge in San Francisco is constantly being painted _____ the tendency of steel to rust with exposure to moisture.

4. The Golden Gate Bridge in San Francisco is constantly being painted

_____ steel tends to rust with exposure to moisture.

5. Bruce Springsteen concerts are always sold out quickly _____
he is such a popular performer.

6. Bruce Springsteen concerts are always sold out quickly _____
his popularity as a performer.

SUMMARY TASK

◆ You are going to write a paragraph describing causes and results.

1. Look at some suggested situations below. Choose one or select one of your own. Make a list of the possible results of being in this situation.

   - Being an only child
   - Being a shy person
   - Not having studied English before going to an English-speaking country
   - Not being comfortable talking to other people

2. Select the results you want to discuss from the list you made.
3. Write a paragraph about the situation you chose.
4. After you have finished, look at your paragraph again.

   - Did you begin with a foundation statement?
   - Do you have grammar links between sentences?
   - Do you have idea links between sentences?

5. Make any revisions you think are necessary before you write your final version.

Main Ideas and Supporting Details

GETTING STARTED

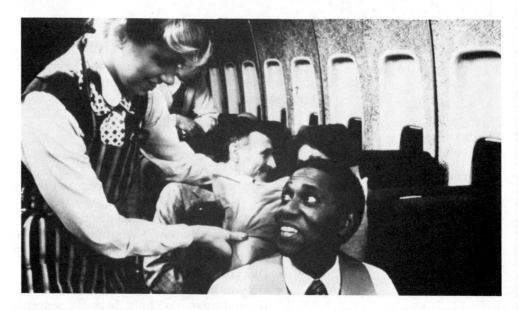

◆ Read the following passage about jet lag. It was originally two paragraphs. Can you find where the first paragraph ends and the second paragraph begins? With a partner, identify the boundary between the two paragraphs and discuss your reasons for making this division.

> Jet lag describes the effect of high-speed jet travel on our bodies' sense of day and night. When our bodies think it is night, it is day, and vice versa. As a result of this internal disarray, travelers who suffer from jet lag feel tired and cranky. Some people can adjust to a three-hour time change in a day, but others take as long as seven days. Because of this jet lag, a trip from the U.S. to Europe or further may take a minimum of two weeks for all body rhythms to become fully synchronized again. There are many ways to minimize the effects of jet lag. One is to schedule arrivals to coincide with your normal bedtime at home and go to sleep soon after arriving. Another is to drink lots of plain fluids on the plane, because dehydration makes the effects of jet lag worse. Avoid caffeine, sweetened soft drinks, and alcohol because they are dehydrating. As smoking and eating big meals on the plane add fatigue and stress on the body, these too should be avoided.

Both paragraphs are about jet lag, but the first one explains what jet lag is and the second describes ways to reduce its effects. A writer can help the reader of a long text by dividing it into paragraphs. A basic principle used to divide paragraphs is that sentences that refer to one topic should be kept together. This topic is usually expressed in a statement of the main idea.

> In this chapter, you will be able to examine how the heart of a paragraph is the main idea and how it is surrounded by supporting details. Together, the heart and its surrounding elements form a paragraph.

◆ **TASK 1.**   Read the passages that follow and determine where the paragraphs should be divided. The number in parenthesis indicates the original number of paragraphs. Compare your divisions with those of another student and talk about how you came to your decisions.

1. Once upon a time, people in the U.S. used to tell stories a lot more than they do now. In earlier days, people were known by the stories they told and the stories that were told about them. Storytelling was a way of passing on family history, of giving meaning to experience, of understanding what happens in people's lives and of passing that knowledge on. Today, television, movies, and books have taken over the once personal and intimate activity of storytelling. We have come to believe that storytelling is for children. However, there are signs that interest in storytelling for adults is returning. (2)

2. Storytelling is an art. It is not reading from a book, and it is not memorizing stories. Although memory is important, the story can grow and change with each new telling. One storyteller always ends her stories by saying, "Take it, and may the next one who tells it, better it." In the history of storytelling, there are two basic types of tellers. The traditional or natural storyteller tells stories about childhood and life experiences. The professional storyteller tells stories about the history and legends of the culture. (2)

TOPICS AND MAIN IDEAS

> The *topics* of the two paragraphs at the beginning of this chapter are about jet lag. The topics in Task 1 are about storytelling. A topic is expressed by a noun or a noun phrase. The *main idea* of the two paragraphs on jet lag is that there are ways to reduce the effects of jet lag. The main idea of the first text in Task 1 is that interest in storytelling for adults is returning. Notice that main ideas are expressed in sentences.

◆ **TASK 2.**   In the following paragraphs, identify the topic and main idea by drawing a circle around each topic and a line under each sentence expressing the main idea. The first one is done for you.

1. (Garlic,) a relative of the onion, can be one of the most satisfying of all seasonings; unfortunately, it is often improperly used. Almost every unpleasant aftereffect of garlic, such as indigestion or bad breath, results from improper preparation. Raw garlic has a sharp sting to the taste. If garlic is fried to a black-brown color, it will be bitter and hard to digest. The mildest garlic flavor is achieved by boiling peeled cloves without browning them.

2. Many people are surprised that the White House, where the president of the United States lives and works, is open to the public. Every day except Sundays, Mondays, and some holidays, guided tours are given to between 6,000 and 8,000 visitors. Public access to the president's home is a U.S. tradition. Even in the middle of the Civil War, in Abraham Lincoln's time, anyone could enter the White House.

3. Although conversation often appears to be without order, it actually follows a set of rules. When people talk to one another, they generally talk one at a time, one after another. When their talk becomes disorganized, that is, when everyone speaks at the same time, or when no one speaks at all, people try to restore order—they stop talking or someone speaks to break the silence.

4. Many American English expressions come from the world of sports. The expression "to start from scratch," which means to start from the very beginning, as in "I baked these cookies from scratch and not from a prepared cookie mix," came from the first Olympic Games, in 776 B.C. At that time, a line scratched in the dirt marked the starting point for foot races and jumping events. One of the richest contemporary sources is baseball. Baseball gave us expressions such as "ballpark figure," which means "an estimate," as in "Can you give me a ballpark figure on how much it would cost to repair my television set?"

SUPPORTING DETAILS

> After identifying the topic and stating the main idea, a writer needs to provide supporting details so that the reader has a good understanding of the main idea.

◆ **TASK 3.**   Look at the second paragraph on jet lag. The main idea is that there are many ways to minimize the effects of jet lag. How many details does the writer give to support this idea? Number these supporting sentences. The first one is done for you.

There are many ways to minimize the effects of jet lag. One is to schedule arrivals to coincide with your normal bedtime at home and go to sleep soon after arriving. Another is to drink lots of plain fluids on the plane, because dehydration makes the effects of jet lag worse. Avoid caffeine, sweetened soft drinks, and alcohol because they are dehydrating. As smoking and eating big meals on the plane add fatigue and stress on the body, these too should be avoided.

◆ **TASK 4.**   Here are two general statements about money and a list of supporting details. Write the number of the general statement next to its supporting statement. Then compare your work with that of another student. The first one is done for you.

GENERAL STATEMENTS

1. Before the invention of coins, many different things were used for money.
2. Money has three uses: it can be used as a medium of exchange, a measure of value, or a way of planning for the future.

Supporting Statements

_2_ Money allows us to compare quite different things, such as a visit to the cinema and a loaf of bread.

____ In North Africa people were paid in salt.

____ People used to exchange goods for other goods.

____ Money allows governments to make budgets.

____ Small shells were used as money in parts of India.

____ Iron was the medium of exchange in West Africa.

____ Money saves us the trouble of bartering for the hundreds of things we need every day.

Selecting Relevant Details

Look at these three general statements from an article on agriculture.

1. Food crops can be divided into grains, fruits, and beverages.

2. As the world's population increases, agriculture grows more important.

3. Farmers have to face problems caused by the weather, by pests, and by diseases.

Notice that without supporting statements, the reader does not learn very much from these general statements.

◆ **TASK 5.** Study the statements which follow. Which of them would you use to support the general statements above? Write the supporting statements in the space for each general statement above. Note that not all of the data may be relevant, that is, they may not have a direct relation to the general statement. Cross out the irrelevant statements, as they will not help support your main idea and may confuse the reader.

- Rice is the major food crop in most of Asia.
- There will be 8 billion mouths to feed by the end of the century.
- Collective farms are found in the USSR.
- Rats eat one-fifth of the world's rice.
- Cotton is an important industrial crop.
- Coffee and tea production provide employment for many in East Africa and India.
- The nations that produce food will be the leading countries of the future.
- Heavy rain can destroy crops.
- Cattle are kept for milk and meat in the U.S.A.
- Oranges are a Mediterranean crop.

◆ **TASK 6.**   With a partner or in a small group, choose one of these main idea statements and make a list of as many supporting statements as you can. Check to see if they are all relevant to the main idea. Eliminate those that are not. Share your list with the rest of the class. Check the lists of the other students for irrelevant supporting details.

1. Animals serve us in many ways.
2. The future of the earth is in danger because of the way people are misusing its resources.
3. Language is more than a means of communication.

Linking Supporting Details

The main idea is the heart of the paragraph. In the previous chapter, a paragraph was compared to a tree. A paragraph can also be compared to the blood system of the body. The main idea is like the heart. The supporting sentences are like the blood vessels. The blood vessels are all linked to the heart. Likewise, supporting sentences are all linked to the main idea.

> After you have made a list of supporting details, you need to decide how to order them and how to link them to each other and to the main idea.

Recall from Chapter 2 that a well-formed paragraph has a structure. The sentences in a paragraph are organized and linked to one another by grammar and idea links.

The main idea statement will often suggest how you can order and link supporting statements. For example, in the paragraph on jet lag in Task 3, the main idea statement suggests that the paragraph be ordered by *listing* ways to minimize jet lag. Notice that the first way is introduced by the word *one;* the second is introduced by *another;* the last example is linked by the word *too.*

◆ **TASK 7.**   Discuss the organization of the following paragraphs. What idea or grammar links did the writer use? What is the main idea in each paragraph? How did the writer order the supporting sentences?

1. Jet lag describes the effect of high-speed jet travel on our bodies' sense of day and night. When our bodies think it is night, it is day, and vice versa. As a result of this internal disarray, travelers who suffer from jet lag feel tired and cranky. Some people can adjust to a three-hour time change in a day, but others take as long as seven days. Because of this

jet lag, a trip from the U.S. to Europe or further may take a minimum of two weeks for all body rhythms to become fully synchronized again.

2. Wind and water are the causes of soil erosion, but both can be controlled by trees. A strong wind can blow away light top soil from an unsheltered field, but trees planted along the side of the field will break the force of the wind. Rain flowing down a hill will cut into the soil and wash it away. Trees not only slow down the flow of water and absorb much of it, they also hold the soil together with their roots.

◆ **TASK 8.**   Now you will practice writing paragraphs.

1. Write a paragraph for statement 1 or 2 in Task 4. Use the relevant supporting statements given, as well as any additional details of your own.
2. Write a paragraph to develop either statement 1, 2, or 3 in Task 6.

SUMMARY TASK

◆ Reexamine the interview you wrote at the end of Chapter One and evaluate it in terms of what you have studied about writing in Chapters 2 and 3.

1. Do you have a main idea statement?
2. Do you have enough supporting details to help your reader understand the main idea?
3. Look at the structure of your paragraphs. Try drawing lines showing the grammar and idea links.
4. How many paragraphs do you have? Should you have divided them differently?
5. Can you see how to improve your interview? Rewrite it using the knowledge you have gained about writing so far.

4 Describing, Comparing, and Contrasting

GETTING STARTED

Suppose you have lost something, let's say a bookbag or briefcase. You call up the Lost and Found Department at your school or office to see if someone has turned it in. Naturally, you will have to describe it. There are many instances in our daily lives when being able to describe something in detail is an invaluable skill. For example:

- You are going to pick up someone who has never seen your car.
- You are going to meet someone at a restaurant, but neither of you has ever seen the other.
- You want to rent a room in your apartment to someone who has never seen it.

◆ Can you think of additional examples of when the ability to describe something clearly would be important? List three more.

In this chapter, you will begin writing different kinds of descriptions.

DESCRIBING OBJECTS

◆ **TASK 1**

A. Let's take the example of the bookbag. If you worked in the Lost and Found Department of a store and someone who had lost a bookbag came looking for it, what details would you need to know? With a partner, list questions that you might ask this person.

B. If the bookbag seeker said, "It's a big red bag with books in it," do you think you would be able to identify the bag? Explain.

C. Look at the description on page 73 in the reference section. Which of your questions does this description answer? Are there answers to other questions that you did not ask?

◆ **TASK 2**

A. Now, let's suppose you want to sell your bookbag. Would you describe it to your possible buyer in the same way? Try writing a description of this bag, which might be posted on a bulletin board.

B. After you have finished your description, compare it with the one on page 73. How are they similar? How are they different?

> Notice that your description will differ depending on the purpose of the description and the intended readers of this description.

◆ **TASK 3.** Think of an object you own. Write two descriptions of it. One is to help you recover the object in case you should lose it. The other is to help you sell it. When you have finished, show your descriptions to a class member and ask this person whether he or she would recognize the object and be interested in buying it. Ask your partner to help you improve your descriptions. Then revise them.

Describing by Comparing and Contrasting

> In describing an object, it is often helpful to compare it with something you think your reader is familiar with.

In the previous example, the bookbag was compared to a suitcase. Some bookbags look like backpacks for hiking. Others look like shopping bags.

Here is another example. To describe comets, early cultures compared them to hair or tails. Today, the most scientifically accurate description of a comet is that it is "like a dirty snowball," because scientists now know that a comet is made up of ice, dust, and gases.

Note that to describe similarities, you can say: *Object X is like object Y,* or *Object X looks like object Y,* as in "A comet *is like* a dirty snowball" or "A comet *looks like* a ball with a tail."

◆ **TASK 4.**   Look at the following list of items. Pick those with which you are familiar. What would you compare them to? Describe as many of these items as you can, or add some of your own.

- a paperback book
- a junior college
- contact lenses
- a streetcar
- a computer

- a helicopter
- falafel
- a wok
- a heart
- a videotape recorder

Comparing Similarities and Differences

> In making comparisons, it is often useful to describe similarities and differences between items. There are many language clues that can help introduce these comparisons.

◆ **TASK 5.**   The italicized expressions in the following four paragraphs describe similarities and differences. Write an *S* above the expressions showing similarities. Write a *D* above the expressions showing differences. The first one is done for you.

1. A class is composed of learners who learn *in different ways.* Some learners like to work in pairs or groups, *whereas* some prefer to work alone. Some learners learn more effectively from people, *while* others learn better from books. Some learners remember what they have heard more easily than what they have read. Some learners seem to learn faster than others, perhaps because they are more willing to make mistakes.

2. Learning a language *is like* learning a skill in many ways. If we compare learning a language to playing tennis, we can appreciate the value of practice. *Both* types of learning require practice. Moreover, we can see how important it is to know exactly what you are practicing and to find out how well you have succeeded in your practice. Learning a skill, such as language use, *is very different from* learning a subject, such as history. We can *neither* rush the process of learning to play tennis *nor* of learning a language, because *both* skills develop over time.

3. Airplanes are more familiar forms of transportation for most people than helicopters, which are used for more specialized purposes. *Although* airplanes can fly faster, they cannot reach places that helicopters can. *Unlike* an airplane, a helicopter does not require a runway and is more maneuverable.

4. Analog computers are measuring computers, *whereas* digital computers are counting computers. The former are *not as* versatile, that is, they cannot perform as many functions, *as* the latter. An example of an analog computer is an ordinary watch, which can do only one thing, that is, tell time. *By contrast,* an electronic watch, which is an example of a digital computer, can tell time, *as well as* act as a miniature calculator or stop watch, and monitor a person's pulse rate.

To check your work, turn to page 74 in the reference section.

Describing Contrasts

> Another way of describing contrasts is to make comparisons using the comparative or superlative form of adjectives and adverbs.

◆ **TASK 6.**   Look at paragraphs 1 and 3 in Task 5. Make a list of the comparative and superlative forms. Then check your work on page 74 in the reference section.

Describing with Relative Clauses

> In Chapter One, you saw that relative clauses are useful devices that allow you to add descriptive information to your writing.

◆ **TASK 7.**   Draw a circle around each of the relative clauses in the paragraphs in Task 5. You should find four of them.

◆ **TASK 8.**   A. Imagine that you have been asked on a chemistry exam to compare characteristics of various substances, such as water and tin. First study the descriptions of the six substances in chart 1 below. Then look at chart 2. For each pair of substances, write a statement describing how they are similar or different according to the point of comparison or contrast. For example, look at point 1. The point of comparison is the *type of element* and the elements to be compared are *helium* and *tin.* One possible statement of comparison is:
   Helium is a gas, whereas tin is a metal.
Another possible statement is:
   Unlike helium, which is a gas, tin is a metal.
Add additional information using relative clauses whenever you can.

CHART 1	
Hydrogen:	An element, atomic weight 1.00797. A colorless, odorless, tasteless gas. The lightest substance known. It is inflammable and combines with oxygen to form water. Occurs in water, in organic compounds and in all living things.
Helium:	An element, atomic weight 4.0026. An inert gas which occurs in certain natural gases in the U.S. in radioactive ores, and in the atmosphere. Non-flammable, very light, valuable for filling airships and balloons.
Tin:	An element, atomic weight 118.69. A silvery-white metal, specific gravity 7.31, melting point 231.85 degrees centigrade, soft, malleable and ductile. The metal is extracted by heating the oxide with powdered carbon. Used for tin-plating and in many alloys.
Mercury:	An element, atomic weight 200.59. A liquid, silvery-white metal, specific gravity 13.6, melting point 39 degrees centigrade, boiling point 357 degrees centigrade. Extracted by roasting the ore in a current of air. Used in thermometers. Alloys used in dentistry. Compounds are poisonous; some are used in medicine.
Sulphuric Acid:	A colorless, oily acid, specific gravity 1.84. Extremely corrosive, reacts violently with water. Used extensively in many processes in the chemical industry.
Water:	The normal oxide of hydrogen. Pure water is a colorless, odorless liquid, melting point 0 degrees centigrade, boiling point 100 degrees centigrade. Has a maximum density of 1.00 grams per cubic centimeter at 4 degrees centigrade.

CHART 2	
Compare	**Point of comparison**
1. Helium and tin	type of substance
2. Mercury and tin	color
3. Hydrogen and water	color and odor
4. Hydrogen and Helium	properties
5. Tin and mercury	melting point
6. Sulphuric acid and mercury	specific gravity
7. Mercury and tin	uses
8. Water and mercury	boiling point

B. After you have finished, compare your statements with those of a classmate. Then group your sentences according to whether they are expressions of similarities or differences.

Qualifying Statements

> As a part of comparing two substances, objects, places, or people, you may want to say that the point of comparison is not necessarily an advantage.

Look at the following example.

> Although airplanes can fly faster, they cannot reach places that helicopters can.

This statement says that it is true airplanes fly faster than helicopters. It also says that this greater speed does not make airplanes better than helicopters because helicopters can reach places airplanes cannot.

Notice how the word *although* is used to qualify the point of comparison. *Although* introduces a subject and a verb and makes the resulting clause a subordinate clause, in the same way that *which* makes the following subject and verb a part of the subordinate, relative clause. When the *although* clause comes first, it tells the reader to expect a qualification to follow in the main clause. Let us look at a few more examples.

> - *Although* Sandra Felton's mother was a "cleanie," Sandra had always been a "messy."
> - *Although* digital computers are more versatile than analog computers, the latter are still useful.

Students sometimes confuse *although* and *but*. Compare the use of these two words in the following examples.

> - *Although* airplanes fly faster than helicopters, they cannot reach places helicopters can.
> - Airplanes fly faster than helicopters, *but* they cannot reach places helicopters can.

There are two main differences between the use of *although* and *but*. One is a grammatical difference. *Although* makes the following subject and verb a part of its subordinate clause. In the first example, a subordinate clause is followed by a main clause. In the second example, there are two main clauses. *But* connects two main clauses. Notice that *although* and *but* do not occur together.

The second difference is in meaning. Remember that main clauses carry the most important information. Therefore, in the first example, the most important information is in the main clause, *they cannot reach places helicopters can.* In the second example, the information in both clauses is equally important. *Although* also tells the reader to expect something different to follow. Let us see if this idea becomes clearer when we try to compare two apartments.

◆ **TASK 9.**   Look at the features of these two apartments. Compare them with a partner. Consider the advantages and disadvantages of each, using qualifying statements to express the idea of positive and negative features. For example, *Although apartment A has no garage, it is close to public transportation.*

Apartment A	Apartment B
• very densely populated area	• small garage
• parking is very difficult	• one-bedroom apartment on the top floor of a modern two-story building
• no garage	
• many restaurants and expensive shops	• close to transportation
• in walking distance of downtown	• 15 minutes by car to school or office; 30 to 45 minutes by bus
• close to transportation	• foggy area of town
• 45 minutes to an hour from the office or school by bus; 20 minutes by car	• many good restaurants in the area
• sunny area of town	• some shops, moderately priced goods
• large studio apartment on the first floor of an old, three-story building	• downtown is accessible by bus
	• quiet, residential area
	• 45 minutes by bus to downtown

SUMMARY TASK

◆ Choose one of the following tasks.

1. Write about a product you would like to buy: running shoes, a watch, etc. Compare two brands. Describe them and indicate which you would buy. Give reasons for your choice.

2. Compare television and radio, or television and the newspaper.

A good way to begin is to list as many ideas as you can. After you have finished, select those ideas that you think will best illustrate your main idea.

Decide what your main idea will be. For example, if you decide to choose the first task, your main idea could be: *Brand X computer is better for my needs than Brand Y.* Then select points that will describe your needs and how Brand X satisfies them better than Brand Y.

As you will recall from earlier chapters, writers typically write many versions of an article or paper. Each version is called a *draft.* Usually writers put their ideas down in the first draft. Then they look at how they have organized them and make changes.

After you have finished your first draft, look at how you have connected your sentences. Determine whether you have divided sentences into paragraphs in the most organized way. Look also to see if you have put important information in main clauses and less important information in subordinate clauses.

Ask a classmate to read your paper and give you suggestions. Then write your final version.

5 Describing Processes, Developments, and Graphs

GETTING STARTED

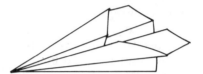

◆ Do you know how to make a paper airplane? Can you describe the steps to someone who does not know how to make one? Take a few minutes to make a paper airplane. Try to describe how you did it.

Now turn to page 74. Match the instructions at the bottom of the page with the pictures at the top of page 75. Then compare your work with a partner's.

In this chapter you will continue to practice writing descriptions. Describing processes, developments, and graphs each has its own way of ordering paragraphs. You will begin to see this order in this chapter.

DESCRIBING PROCESSES

The first step in planning a description of a process, such as making a paper airplane, is to list the main steps in the order that the process should be completed. The next step is to decide how to identify the sequence of events so that they are clear to the reader.

For example, here is one way someone might describe the process of making a paper airplane.

First, you will need a sheet of paper that is 8 1/2 by 11 inches. Fold it in half lengthwise. *Next,* open the paper and fold one corner toward the center crease. *After you have made* the first fold, fold the other corner down, in the same way, along the dotted line. *Then,* fold each side along the diagonal dotted line toward the center. *Now,* turn the paper over. With the paper turned over, fold one side over along the dotted line. *Next,* fold the other side along the other dotted line. *The last step* is to tape the body of the plane together. You now have a paper airplane that is ready for a test flight!

The italicized words and phrases mark the sequence of the process. They help the reader follow the process the writer is describing. They make the transition from one idea to the next, from one sentence to the next, easier to follow than if they were not there.

Notice that the words *first, next, then,* and *now* are simply added to the sentence, and are followed by commas. *The first/next/last step* are noun phrases that function as the subject of the sentence. They must be followed by a form of the verb *be. After* marks a subordinate clause, that is, a subject and a verb, which must be followed by a main clause.

Marking Sequence

Look at the following list. It shows some of the language that is useful for marking sequence.

To mark the beginning:
First, . . .   The first step is . . .   The first thing you do is . . .

To mark the next step:
Next, . . .   The next step is . . .

To mark following steps:
Then, . . .   After this step, . . .   After you do this, . . .   Now, . . .

To show the last step:
Finally, . . .   The last step is . . .

◆ **TASK 1.**   Look at this illustration of how to put in contact lenses. An illustration can show the steps of a process clearly by using pictures and numbering these pictures. Without these pictures and numbers, a written description must make these steps clear by using expressions that show sequence. Write a description of how to put in contact lenses.

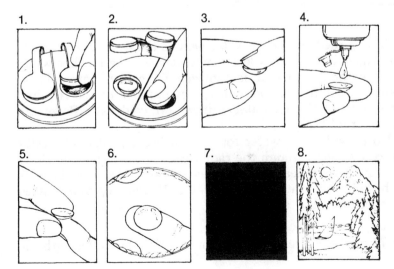

How to Put in Contact Lenses

1. Open lens case.
2. Remove lens by touching it with your right index finger.
3. Grasp lens with thumb and index finger of your left hand.
4. Apply one drop of wetting solution to concave surface.
5. Place lens on right index finger, concave side up.
6. Use middle fingers of the left and right hand to hold eye open. Touch lens to cornea.
7. Blink.
8. Enjoy the scenery. Life is beautiful with contact lenses.

Describing Processes with the Passive Voice

The passive voice is used in the description of a process or development when the agent—the person performing the action—is not important.

◆ **TASK 2.** Look at the following diagram illustrating the flow of water through a house. Read the description of this process. There are five examples of the passive voice. Underline each one of these examples.

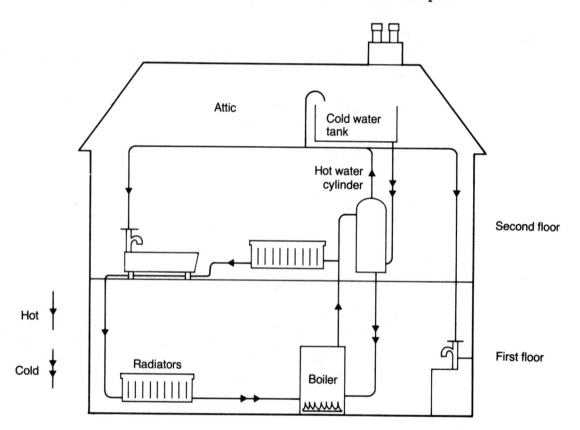

The boiler is first turned on. As the water next to the heat source warms up, it expands. Because hot water is less dense, it rises. As the hot water rises into the hot water cylinder, it is replaced by cooler water. These movements continue until all the water in the cylinder is at the required temperature. When some of the hot water is drawn off, cold water flows into the cylinder from the roof tank.

The boiler also provides hot water for central heating. As this water heats, it rises by convection through the radiators. As the hot water flows through the radiators, it loses heat and becomes denser, and so it sinks back to the boiler. In the boiler the water is again heated. Usually a pump is fitted to the system to speed the flow of hot water.

Look at page 75 in the reference section for additional practice with the passive voice.

DESCRIBING DEVELOPMENTS

> Describing developments usually involves organizing your information into main stages, or main events, and showing the time relationship between these events.

◆ **TASK 3.** The time line below shows the stages in the development of an imaginary African city. Refer to the time line and try to guess when each of the events occurred. Write the date or dates in the spaces provided. For example, we can assume that the earliest date, 868, indicates when the city was founded, and that between 868 and 1550 Arabic was the most important language.

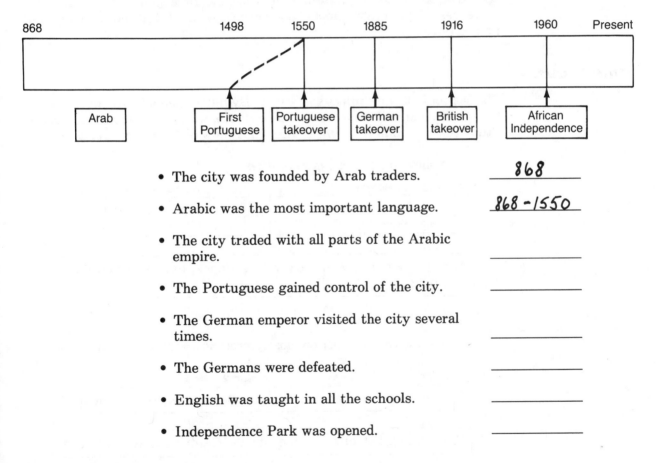

- The city was founded by Arab traders.   *868*

- Arabic was the most important language.   *868 - 1550*

- The city traded with all parts of the Arabic empire.   _____

- The Portuguese gained control of the city.   _____

- The German emperor visited the city several times.   _____

- The Germans were defeated.   _____

- English was taught in all the schools.   _____

- Independence Park was opened.   _____

Time Relationships

> In describing developments, time relationships are important. A writer can show the sequence of events by using time prepositions or time clauses.

Prepositions of Time

You can show the sequence of events by using prepositions of time. Look at how the italicized prepositions are used in the following examples.

> - *In* 868, the city was founded by Arab traders.
> - *During* the German period, German was taught in all schools.
> - *After* 1916, the British controlled the city.
> - *Between* 1550 and 1885, the city felt the influence of the Portuguese.
> - The first Portuguese arrived *in* 1498, but they did not take over the city *until* 1550.
> - The Germans controlled the city *from* 1885 *to* 1916.

◆ **TASK 4.** Use the information from the time line in Task 2. Write sentences of your own about the development of this city, using time prepositions.

Time Clauses

Clauses consist of a subject and a verb. By putting an adverb of time before the subject and verb, you create a time clause, which is a subordinate clause. Study these examples of time clauses that show different time relationships.

1. To show sequence: *before* or *after*

Action 1	**Action 2**
Africans won their independence.	Independence Park was built.

> After the Africans won their independence, Independence Park was built.

2. To show that one action closely preceded another action: *when*

Action 1	**Action 2**
The British attacked the city.	The Germans were driven out.

> When the British attacked the city, the Germans were driven out.

3. To show that two actions are happening at the same time: *as*

Action 1	The number of Portuguese increased.
Action 2	The power of the Arabs was reduced.

> As the number of Portuguese increased, the power of the Arabs was reduced.

4. To show an action and its limit: *until*

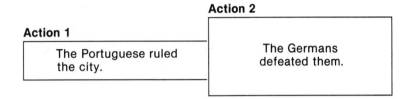

> The Portuguese ruled the city until the Germans defeated them.

When time clauses come at the beginning of a sentence, they are followed by a comma (,). For example:

> Until the Germans defeated them, the Portuguese ruled the city.

◆ **TASK 5.**　This exercise has two parts.

A. First connect each pair of sentences according to the relationship symbolized by boxes.　For example:

> | The Wright brothers flew the first airplane in 1908. | A new age of flying began. |

> When the Wright brothers flew the first airplane in 1908, a new age of flying began.

1.
> | The century progressed. |
> | Longer and longer distances were covered. |

2.
> | The Second World War ended. | Jet airliners were built. |

3.
> | Man had flown only in balloons. | The Wright brothers made their first flight. |

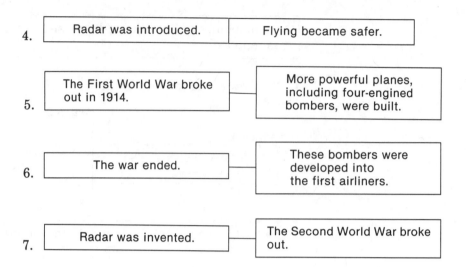

4. | Radar was introduced. | Flying became safer. |

5. | The First World War broke out in 1914. | More powerful planes, including four-engined bombers, were built. |

6. | The war ended. | These bombers were developed into the first airliners. |

7. | Radar was invented. | The Second World War broke out. |

B. Now put the completed sentences in a logical order and combine them into a paragraph. Feel free to add examples and further details of your own to improve the paragraph. When you have finished, compare your work with a classmate's.

DESCRIBING GRAPHS

Graphs are a way of showing change visually. They are often used in physics, the life sciences, economics, and social sciences, and are an economic way of presenting information. Take, for example, the graph below, which shows the average number of cigarettes smoked per person in a European country over a period of 60 years.

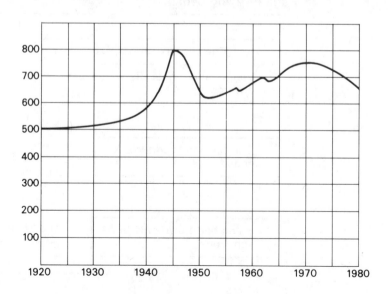

◆ **TASK 6.** A. With a partner, look at the graph of cigarette smoking. Try to describe the graph for the following periods:

1. 1920–1930 2. 1945–1950 3. 1956–1958 4. 1968–1972

B. Compare your sentences with those of others in your class. Then look at page 77 in the reference section for practice with language used to describe change.

◆ **TASK 7.** Try to guess the reasons for some of the changes in the graph. You might begin by thinking about general reasons for increases or decreases in smoking. After you have finished making your list of reasons, compare them with the ones suggested on page 79 in the reference section.

◆ **TASK 8.** Write a paragraph describing the graph of cigarette smoking. Include reasons for the changes. In writing your paragraph, you may want to refer to Chapter 3 and the description of writing about causes and reasons.

◆ **TASK 9.** Look at the three charts below. What do they tell you? Write as many statements as you can, based on the information given in these charts. Compare your statements with those of another student.

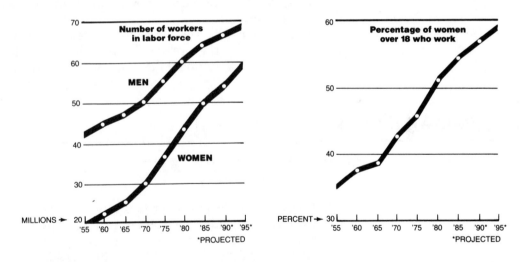

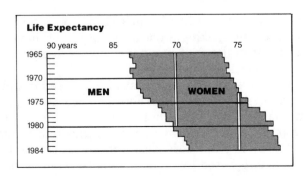

◆ **TASK 10.** In this task you are going to write a paragraph about women in the work force by referring to graphs and other facts. How will you go about doing this?

A. Consider the following. Economists predict severe labor shortages in the 1990s. Look at the graphs in Task 9 again. The graphs tell you three important things about women that could offer a solution to this shortage. What are they?

B. Look at the following facts about women and work in the United States.

- More than half of all mothers work.
- There is no national day-care system.
- There is a shortage of competent, affordable child care services.
- No more than 40% of working women have any form of maternity leave.
- Many companies do not guarantee that a woman will get her job back when she returns from a leave.

What do you think the consequences of these facts will be on women and work?

C. Write a paragraph in which you describe the role of women in solving the labor shortage.

- Begin your paragraph by explaining the reasons why the feminization of the work force is important, citing the information from the graphs.
- Then explain why the increased presence of women may not be the solution to the predicted labor shortage. Refer to the facts above, or any additional information you may have.

SUMMARY TASK

◆ Select one of the following tasks.

1. Describe a process.
2. Describe the development of a city.
3. Describe the major developments in your own life. To help in this task, draw a timeline to represent your life and mark the significant dates in your life on this timeline.

By now, it should not be a surprise that you will need to write more than one draft. Begin by making a list of steps, if you have chosen to describe a process, or a list of dates, if you have chosen to describe the developments. Add as many details as you can.

After you have written your first draft, reread it and see if you can make it clearer by using sequence markers or time clauses. Check to see if you have made clear connections from one sentence to the next. Make any of the changes you feel would improve your writing. Ask a classmate to read your description and tell you if it is clear and understandable. Make any changes that might be suggested by your classmate. Then write a final version.

Writing Explanations

GETTING STARTED

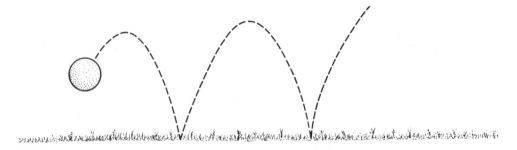

Why does a ball bounce?

◆ Write an answer to this question. Compare your answer with that of another student. Then read the description in the reference section on page 79 . Were you satisfied with your answer? If not, why not?

> Being able to give a clear explanation is a valuable skill. In this chapter, you will have the opportunity to practice giving explanations.

PLANNING AN EXPLANATION

Explanations are answers to questions that ask *why*. Explanations can also be answers to questions about cause and effect.

Consider a small sample of such questions.

* Why do people snore? (Or, what causes people to snore?)
* Why is the world climate changing? (Or, what has caused the world climate to change?)
* Why is English such an important language in the world today? (Or, what are some reasons English is such an important language in the world today? What has caused English to become such an important language today?)
* How can airplanes fly? (Or, what causes airplanes to fly?)

> When you plan an explanation, you need to consider:
>
> 1. Your readers. What do your readers already know about the topic and what do they need to know?
> 2. Supporting information. What kind of information do you need to support your explanation—definitions, descriptions, reasons, causes, effects? How much supporting information do you need to provide an effective explanation?

◆ **TASK 1.** Study these explanations. Is there enough supporting information in each one? If not, what does the reader need to know in order to understand them?

1. Snoring is caused by obstructive breathing during sleep.
2. Airplanes fly because their wings give them lift and their engines provide the force to produce thrust.

If your reader is unfamiliar with the topic, you as the writer, need to provide sufficient information to help the reader understand it. You may need to include definitions or descriptions of words that the reader may not know. For example, in sentence 1, you may want to define *obstructive* for the reader: *Snoring is obstructive breathing during sleep, that is, something blocks the airway during sleep.*

EXPLANATIONS WITH INSTRUCTIONS

> When giving instructions, it is sometimes helpful to include explanations so that people understand the reasons for the instructions and will follow them carefully.

◆ **TASK 2.** Look at the following instructions for victims of poisoning. Underline the sentences which give explanations.

1. If the victim is not breathing, give her artificial respiration immediately. Lack of oxygen can cause brain damage within three minutes.
2. If she seems likely to vomit, place her on her stomach with her head to one side so that she will not inhale any vomit that might choke her.
3. If she is conscious, ask her what she has taken. Look for bottles, tablets, or the smell of any chemical, as this will make it easier to identify the poison and start the correct treatment.
4. Keep her warm to limit the effects of shock.
5. Do not leave her before the doctor arrives because her condition may worsen quickly.

Notice the language used to provide the explanations above.

1. A new sentence explains the effect of not giving artificial respiration right away.
2. The phrase *so that* introduces the reason for placing the victim on her stomach with her head to one side.
3. The word *as* introduces the reason for looking for evidence of the poison.
4. *To* (a short form of *in order to*) introduces the reason for keeping the victim warm.
5. *Because* introduces the reason for remaining with the victim.

◆ **TASK 3.**   Read this paragraph which gives instructions for a simple experiment to prove that water expands when it is frozen. With a partner, try to answer the questions in parentheses so as to give explanations for the different steps of the experiment. When you have agreed on the answers, rewrite the paragraph to include the explanations. Use the language described in Task 2 to help you.

A very simple experiment can be done to show that water expands when it is frozen. All you need is an empty glass jar. (*Why?*) Fill half the jar with water. (*Why?*) Then mark the water level on the outside of the jar. (*Why?*) After that, put the jar in a freezer. (*Why?*) When the water is frozen, take the jar out of the freezer and observe the new water level. You will see that the level of the frozen water is higher. (*Why?*)

◆ **TASK 4.**   Look at the activities below. Choose one and write instructions for it. Be sure to include explanations with your instructions. When you have finished, compare them with those of another student who has written on the same topic. Ask the other student to explain any points you do not understand.

1. Minimizing jet lag
2. Finding an apartment
3. Making a paper airplane
4. Putting in contact lenses
5. Learning a foreign language
6. Cultivating a vegetable garden

SUPPORTING AN EXPLANATION

Compare these two pairs of statements. Which pair works better as a general statement and supporting statement? Why?

a. Studying in a small school is better than studying in a large school. A small school has fewer students.
b. Studying in a small school is better than studying in a large school. In a small school, students can get more individual attention from teachers.

In **a**, the second statement simply rephrases the first. In **b**, the second statement gives additional information, explaining why the small school is better than the large. For this reason, the second statement in **b** effectively serves as a supporting statement, whereas the second statement in **a** does not.

◆ **TASK 5.** Which supporting statement **a** or **b**, would you use to explain each of these statements? Discuss the reason for your choice with a partner.

1. Many towns grew up near rivers.
   a. London, New York, and Amsterdam were built on river banks.
   b. The river provided water, transport, and later, power.

2. Wood is a useful building material.
   a. Wood is used for doors, roofs, and floors.
   b. For its weight, wood is exceptionally strong.

3. Fruit and vegetables are essential for health.
   a. Fruit and vegetables contain vitamin C.
   b. Ships always carry supplies of fruit and vegetables to keep the crew healthy.

4. Much of North Africa is desert.
   a. Very little rain falls in North Africa.
   b. Very little will grow in North Africa.

5. Gold was used for money in many parts of the world.
   a. Gold is a rare metal and it does not corrode.
   b. Gold coins were made in Europe, Asia, and America.

◆ **TASK 6.** *Wildlife is declining*. Choose statements from the list below to explain this fact. Write a paragraph of explanation using statements in the list together with others of your own.

   1. There are only 2,000 tigers in Asia.
   2. The jungle everywhere is being cleared.
   3. There are over 100 animals which may disappear in the next 25 years.
   4. Chemicals that are used to kill insects are affecting birds.
   5. Diseases like malaria, which kept people out of the jungle, have been conquered.
   6. Some kinds of whale are almost extinct.
   7. The world's growing population needs more and more land.
   8. Some wild animals, such as the whale, are being overhunted.

◆ **TASK 7.** Someone from your class is planning to visit your native country. What five places would you recommend that this person visit? Write a paragraph recommending these places with at least one supporting reason that explains why each place would be interesting to visit.

CAUSE AND EFFECT IN EXPLANATIONS

Drinking alcoholic beverages is a common practice in many countries. Excessive and habitual drinking, or alcoholism, is a problem in many of these countries. Why is this a problem? What are some of the effects of alcoholism on society? Before answering this question, work through the following tasks.

◆ **TASK 8.** With a partner, make a list of some of the effects of alcoholism on society. Make a composite list of effects, combining yours with those of the rest of the class.

◆ **TASK 9.** What is the relationship between the following: impaired driving, accidents, drinking too much alcohol, and drunkenness? Fill in the diagram below to illustrate this relationship.

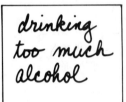 Leads to →  Leads to →  Leads to →

Talking About Cause and Effect

Notice the italicized words in the examples below. These words will help you talk about cause and effect. Some of these expressions are used when the cause is mentioned first in the sentence, as in, "*Drunk drivers* cause accidents." The others are used when the effect is mentioned first, as in, "*Many accidents* are caused by drunk drivers."

1. If you want to mention the *cause* first:

Cause		Effect
Drunk drivers	*cause*	accidents.
Drunk drivers	*are the cause of*	many accidents.
Drunk driving	*results in*	accidents.

2. If you want to mention the *effect* first:

Effect		Cause
Many accidents	*are caused by*	drunk drivers.
Many accidents occur	*because of*	drunk drivers.
Many accidents occur	*because*	people drive while they are drunk.
Many accidents	*are the result of*	drunk driving.

◆ **TASK 10.** Select one of the effects of alcoholism from the list you compiled for Task 8. Write three different statements of cause and effect, mentioning the cause first. Then write four different statements of cause and effect, mentioning the effect first. Follow the examples on page 45. Share your statements with the class.

Talking about Possible Cause and Effect

A statement such as "Drinking too much alcohol *causes* alcoholism" asserts that drinking too much alcohol *always* causes alcoholism. We can modify this statement to mean that alcoholism is a *possible* result of drinking too much alcohol this way:

> Drinking too much alcohol *may cause* alcoholism.

An effect may have several causes or a cause may have more than one effect. Adding *may* allows us to express this idea of multiple causes or effects. For example:

> Accidents *may occur* because people drive while they are drunk. However, accidents *may* also *occur* because of bad weather conditions, careless drivers, or mechanical problems.

In some cases, the word *cause* may not be appropriate because the relationship between two events is not direct. For example, drinking too much alcohol may not cause alcoholism. It may only result in a hangover, nausea, or abnormal behavior. We may then choose to use a different verb, such as *lead to*. For example:

> Drinking too much alcohol *leads to* alcoholism.

We can add *may* to this sentence to indicate the possibility of the result. For example:

> Drinking too much alcohol *may lead to* alcoholism.

◆ **TASK 11.** Look at the list of items below. The items in the left column may be causes or effects of the items in the right column, but the items are mixed up.

malaria	drought
mental stress	heavy rain and strong winds
icy conditions	mosquito bites
soil erosion	road accidents
lack of rain	overcrowding
juvenile delinquency	loud noise
deafness	broken homes

A. First, match the words in the two columns. Then, determine the relationship between each pair. For example, *malaria* and *mosquito bites* form a pair. Mosquito bites are the cause; malaria is the effect.

B. Write a statement about each pair, making the item in the left column the subject of your sentence. Choose a verb that is appropriate, adding *may* if needed. For example, *Malaria is caused by mosquito bites.*

C. Next, write a statement about each pair, making the item in the right column the subject of your sentence. For example, *Mosquito bites cause malaria.*

Linking Cause and Effect

Why does the wind blow from the sea to the land during the day? Look at this diagram.

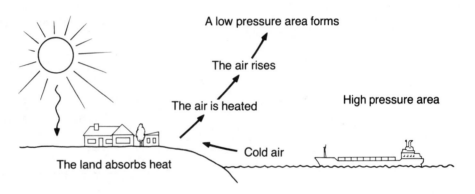

The explanation consists of a series of cause and effect steps. Here are some of them:

1. The land absorbs heat from the sun.
2. The air above the land becomes hot.
3. The heated air expands and rises.
4. An area of low pressure forms over the land. (When air rises, an area of low pressure is formed.)
5. Cold air from the high pressure over the sea flows in. (Air flows from high to low pressure areas.)

◆ **TASK 12.** Underline the expressions that show the cause and effect relationship between the events in the two paragraphs below. The first one is done for you.

A. Why does the wind blow from the sea to the land during the day? During the day, the land absorbs heat from the sun and heats the air above it. The heated air expands and rises. This <u>causes</u> a low pressure area <u>to</u> form. Because the cold air above the sea forms a high pressure area, and air flows from high to low pressure areas, the air above the sea will flow toward the land.

B. Why does the wind blow from the sea to the land during the day? The land absorbs heat from the sun during the day. As a result, the air above the land is heated. When air, which is a gas, is heated, it expands and rises. This forms an area of low pressure. The cold air above the sea forms a high pressure area. Air flows from high pressure to low pressure areas; therefore, the air above the sea blows toward the land.

Did you find the following expressions: *because, therefore, as a result, cause . . . to?* Notice that *because* introduces a cause. It connects two clauses. *Therefore* introduces an effect. It connects two sentences. To combine two sentences using *therefore,* use a semicolon before the word and a comma after it. *As a result* functions like *therefore.* Notice with the verb *cause,* which introduces an effect, the preposition *to* is used.

◆ **TASK 13.** Study this diagram. Then write an explanation of why the wind blows from the land to the sea during the night.

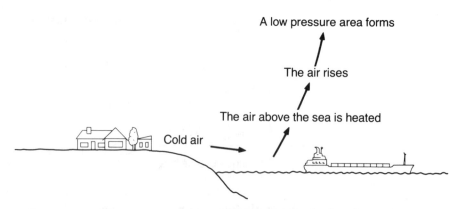

A low pressure area forms

The air rises

The air above the sea is heated

Cold air

The sea retains the heat longer than the land

SUMMARY TASK

◆ Write an explanation of a problem or an answer to a *why* question that you think would be interesting to your classmates or to your friends at home. Here are some suggestions.

1. Why are students from my country quiet/outspoken in class?
2. Why are students from my country good at language learning?
3. Why do Americans travel by car more than by any other form of transportation?
4. Why do so many/so few students from my country study in the United States?
5. Why is alcoholism/suicide/drunk driving a problem in my country?

Writing Arguments

GETTING STARTED

◆ Look at the following list of careers. Choose one of them and list as many reasons as you can to persuade another student to pursue one of them.

1. lawyer
2. actor
3. writer
4. photographer
5. teacher
6. model
7. obstetrician
8. computer scientist
9. artist
10. musician

Now give your list to another student, who will try to argue against each point you made. Examine your partner's replies and consider how your argument could be improved.

To produce an effective argument, you need to consider:

1. Your supporting statements.
   Are they opinions only?
   Are there enough statements to convince your readers?
   Have you accounted for the opposite point of view?

2. Your readers.
   Who are they?
   What do they know about your topic?
   How do they feel about your topic?
   How do they feel about you?

3. The organization of your argument.

In this chapter, you will have a chance to practice writing arguments with each of these points in mind.

SUPPORTING AN ARGUMENT

The first step in planning an argument is to list the points you wish to make. Some of these may be *facts*. Some may be *opinions*. Facts are statements which are known to be true. Opinions are personal beliefs, which may or may not be true. Both facts and opinions are used in arguments, but it is important to distinguish between them. Your reader will not be easily convinced by an argument consisting only of opinions.

Facts and Opinions

◆ **TASK 1.** Suppose that your parents would like you to get a Ph.D. in computer science. They give you the following reasons why you should follow their advice.

1. Your mother has a Ph.D. in computer science.
2. Computers are everywhere; life in the present and the future cannot function without computers, so it will be easy to get a job.
3. Computer scientists are well paid.
4. According to a study completed by the head of the computer science department of a major university, the demand for doctorate holders in computer science in 1987 was more than 1,000; the supply was 325.
5. In this same study, starting salaries at most major companies is estimated to be around $50,000 a year.
6. A researcher at a manufacturer of computer systems says that computer science is an expanding field. He is free to experiment and try new things in his research, and he is really glad to be doing it.

Which of the reasons above are opinions and which are facts? Which ones are more persuasive? Why?

The Rule of Relevance

> Each statement in support of an argument should be relevant to the argument; in other words, it should have a direct connection to the issue.

◆ **TASK 2.** In pairs or small groups, decide which of the following statements are relevant to the argument below. Then compare your choices with your classmates'.

> Smoking is harmful to society.

1. People smoke much more when they are worried.
2. Smoking is a waste of resources.
3. Smokers have caused fires which have resulted in heavy damage to property, and even death.
4. Smokers are thoughtless people.
5. Smokers cause health problems for themselves and for others.
6. The tobacco industry is an important part of the American economy.

The Weight of Authority

In the arguments presented in favor of computer science as a field of study, the salary figure from the computer scientist's study carries more weight than the statement that computer scientists make more money.

> Authority can come from facts in a study, or it can come from the importance of an individual.

◆ **TASK 3.**   Look at the next argument and the statements listed below. Identify each as personal experience or outside authority. Do all of the statements support the argument? Which ones do and which ones do not?

> Eating breakfast is necessary for better health and performance.

1. My mother always told me if I didn't eat breakfast, I wouldn't have enough energy for the day's activities.
2. If I don't eat breakfast, I feel tired all day.
3. A study of 50 people done by the University of Iowa over 30 years ago showed that both mental and physical performance were improved by eating breakfast.
4. A friend of mine never eats breakfast and says it hasn't bothered him at all.
5. In 1982, a British nutritionist studied 500 children and concluded that there was no statistical difference between those who ate breakfast and those who didn't.
6. Joan Benoit, the 1984 winner of the Olympic women's marathon, eats a meal after she runs at the beginning of the day. If she gets an early start, the meal is breakfast. If not, the meal is brunch.

Elaborating on an Argument

◆ **TASK 4.**   Read the following argument against prisons.

Putting lawbreakers into prison is an unsatisfactory way of dealing with those who break the law for two reasons. First, it does not deter an individual from committing crimes again once he or she leaves prison. Second, imprisonment may be an ineffective form of punishment. Alternative methods of dealing with lawbreakers must be explored.

Now that you have read this argument, are you convinced? Which of the details below elaborate on the first argument? Which ones elaborate on the second?

1. More than 35% of all prisoners break the law again after their release from prison.

2. Prisoners are allowed visitors and have access to libraries and sports facilities.
3. Prisons are overcrowded.
4. Young prisoners often meet more experienced criminals and learn from them.
5. Prisoners are sometimes, themselves, victims of crime in prison.
6. Prisoners can take classes, as well as work and earn a small sum of money while in prison.

Let us see what the revised argument looks like.

Putting lawbreakers into prison is an unsatisfactory way of dealing with those who break the law for two reasons. First, it does not deter an individual from committing crimes again once he or she leaves prison. Young prisoners often meet more experienced criminals and learn from them. Moreover, prisoners, themselves, are sometimes victims of crime in prison. More than 35% of all prisoners break the law again after their release from prison. Second, imprisonment may be an ineffective form of punishment. Prisoners are allowed visitors and have access to libraries and sports facilities. In addition, they can take classes and work and earn a small sum of money. Alternative methods for dealing with lawbreakers must be explored.

> By elaborating on your reasons, you give your reader more information; as a result, your reader may be more willing to agree with your point of view.

Useful Language for Presenting Supporting Details

Notice in the paragraph above how the number of reasons is given at the beginning: "Putting lawbreakers into prison is an unsatisfactory way of dealing with those who break the law *for two reasons*." Notice also how each reason is identified by an ordinal number, *first* and *second*, and how *moreover* and *in addition* are used to elaborate on supporting details.

◆ **TASK 5.** Complete the following sets of statements with an additional supporting detail of your own. Then link the statements in each set together, using either *moreover* or *in addition*.

1. Education for women is a waste of time.
   a. Most women become housewives.
   b.

2. Education for women is essential.
   a. Women have the greatest influence on the family.
   b.

3. A woman would be an effective head of government.
   a. Women prefer to work out problems through communication than to be confrontational
   b.

4. Everyone in the world should learn English.
   a. It is already a major language of trade.
   b.

5. Children are responsible for the welfare of their elderly parents.
   a. Their parents cared for them when they were children.
   b.

CONSIDERING YOUR AUDIENCE

Read the following argument against banning smoking. Which of the audiences in the list below do you think it is intended for? How many reasons are given? How many reasons are opinions? How many are facts? Are all the reasons relevant?

I do not recommend banning smoking on this airline as long as every airline has a choice to enforce or not to enforce such a rule. As many passengers who smoke will be upset by such a rule, particularly if the flight is a long one, we will lose their business to other airlines that do not have a no-smoking rule. One airline has already tried to encourage passengers to refrain from smoking on a voluntary basis and rewarded them with a coupon for a discount on a subsequent flight. Many passengers chose to smoke rather than to get the discount. At present, we have separate sections for smokers and non-smokers. This is a sufficient accommodation to the non-smoking passengers. A change to a complete ban will negatively affect our company financially.

1. hotel managers
2. airline officials
3. health insurance companies
4. employers
5. cigarette companies
6. school officials

◆ **TASK 6.** Divide into pairs or small groups. Choose one of the audiences above. Write an argument to support a ban on smoking in public places. After you have finished, read your argument to another group that will identify your intended audience, identify the number of reasons you came up with, evaluate each one for relevance, and identify each as opinion or fact.

◆ **TASK 7.** In small groups, plan a campaign to support a law which would require all automobile drivers and their passengers to wear seatbelts. Here are some suggestions that might help you get started.

1. Think of as many supporting reasons as you can.

2. Consider the points of view of various groups of people, such as drivers, passengers, fat people, lazy people, insurance companies, police officers, lawmakers, doctors, parents, children. How do you think they would feel about such a law? Would they support or oppose it? If they would oppose it, can you think of arguments that might change their minds?

3. Interview three people outside of class about their opinions of such a law. Write down their statements as well as any supporting details they provide.

4. Now, review your list of supporting details. Include the arguments from your interviews, if they are relevant. Eliminate any details that are irrelevant. Determine if you have a sufficient number of details to convince your audience. If not, add more. Save this list for later work.

ORGANIZING AN ARGUMENT

A good argument is organized so that a reader can easily follow it. Here are two possible ways of organizing an argument. The first way is to begin with your reasons and end with your conclusion, that is, the statement of your argument. The second way is to begin with your conclusion followed by your supporting reasons.

◆ **TASK 8.** Read the two arguments below. Which one uses the first method? Which one uses the second method?

A. Airplanes are small, enclosed areas. Separating the cabin of a plane into smoking and non-smoking areas does little to prevent the smoke from reaching all parts of the airplane. This is significant, given the fact that the surgeon general of the United States, the highest medical officer in the country, has taken a position against smoking as hazardous to health. Moreover, it has been established that smoking is not only a danger to the smokers' health, but the smoke exhaled is dangerous to those around the smoker as well. Therefore, it is essential that smoking on planes be completely banned.

B. It is essential that smoking be completely banned on airplanes. For one thing, airplanes are small, enclosed areas. Separating the cabin of a plane into smoking and non-smoking areas does little to prevent the smoke from reaching all parts of the airplane. In addition, the surgeon general of the United States, the highest medical officer in the country, has taken a position against smoking as hazardous to health. Moreover, it has been established that smoking is not only a danger to the smoker's health, but the smoke exhaled is dangerous to those around the smoker as well.

Summarizing an Argument

Notice the use of *therefore* in paragraph A above to signal the concluding statement.

Some other expressions you can use to let your reader know that you are ending or summarizing your argument are listed below.

- *For these reasons,*
- *As a result,*
- *Thus,*
- *Finally,*
- *In conclusion,*

◆ **TASK 9.**   As a class, identify the sentence which states the argument. Then organize the statements in the two ways described above, ending with the argument statement or beginning with it.

1. Dogs carry disease.
2. Pet dogs should be banned.
3. Dogs are dangerous to man.
4. Dogs may attack people.
5. Pet dogs eat lots of food.
6. Dogs are expensive to keep.
7. People buy beds and toys for dogs.

◆ **TASK 10.**   In small groups, identify the argument statement. Then order the statements. Write a paragraph linking them with the organizational signals discussed in this unit, such as, *moreover, in conclusion.*

1. Success in exams depends on the student performing well on one day only.
2. Exams cause great anxiety.
3. The examination system should be changed.
4. The student is not given credit for good work done throughout the year.
5. Some students do not perform well because they are anxious.

REFUTING AN ARGUMENT

When you want to refute an argument—that is, argue against it—you should consider its weak points. It is not enough to argue against the main points only. You should also try to argue against supporting reasons.

◆ **TASK 11.** Read the following paragraph. Then look at the diagram which shows the structure of this paragraph.

Many people believe that eating carrots improves night vision. Without a sufficient amount of vitamin A, the body cannot process the chemicals needed for night vision. Carrots are an especially good source of carotene, the vegetable substance which may be converted into vitamin A in the body. However, it is unlikely that carrots alone can improve eyesight. Vegetables lag far behind animal sources of vitamin A such as liver, butter, and milk. Few Americans have vision problems stemming strictly from low vitamin A levels and, consequently, boosting carrot consumption in order to see better at night probably will not have much effect.

Complete the diagram with sentences from the paragraph. The first few sentences are done for you.

STRUCTURE OF A PARAGRAPH REFUTING AN ARGUMENT

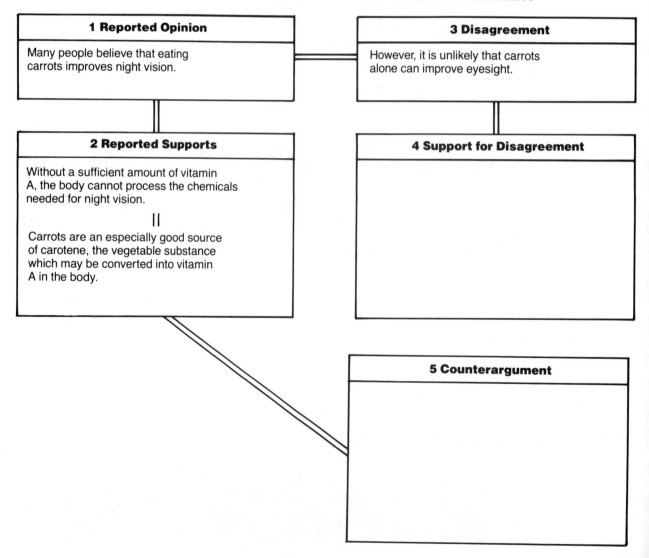

◆ **TASK 12.** Read the following sentences. Order them according to the diagram in Task 11. Then rewrite the sentences in paragraph form. The first one is done for you.

_____ They say that we would all fall off if it were round.

_____ We do not fall off because we are held to the Earth by gravity.

_1_ Members of the Flat Earth Society claim that the Earth is flat.

_____ This is nonsense.

_____ We know that the world is round because if we travel far enough in one direction, we will eventually arrive back where we started.

Compare your paragraph with the one on page 79 in the reference section.

Supporting your Refutation

> Whether you are arguing for or against a position, your arguments are made stronger if you support them with relevant facts and opinions.

◆ **TASK 13.** Earlier in this unit you planned a campaign to support a mandatory seat belt law.

A. Look at the following facts and opinions. Which ones could you use in your campaign? Which ones would be used as counterarguments?

1. The government has no business interfering with the individual rights of its citizens.
2. A study by the University of North Carolina determined that seat belts reduced serious injuries by up to 50 percent and fatal injuries by as much as 75 percent.
3. In New York, traffic deaths declined 17 percent in 1985, the first year that the state's mandatory seat belt law was in effect.
4. In numerous fatal crashes, people wearing seat belts have been trapped inside their cars when the cars caught fire.
5. Seat belts are only necessary on highways at high speeds.
6. 80 percent of all accidents and serious injuries occur in cities at speeds of less than 40 miles per hour.

B. Read the following paragraph. Is the writer for or against a mandatory seat belt law? What facts or opinions does the writer use to support the argument?

Opponents of a mandatory seat belt law argue that the government has no business interfering with our civil rights; however, laws that protect people are not laws which violate basic rights. In fact, we have many laws that govern drivers for the good of all. For example, anyone who wishes to drive must have a license and, if needed, wear glasses while driving.

The Language of Refutation

Notice in the paragraph above that the writer first states the opposing view (*Opponents argue that....*), and then lists the counterarguments (*however,....*).

To show that the writer does not personally hold the opinions that are refuted, these opinions are often introduced as reported speech, using a phrase or verb, as in the following examples:

Some people	*argue*	*that ...*
	say	
	assert	
	believe	
	claim	
	are of the opinion	

The counterargument is often introduced by a phrase showing disagreement, such as:

```
This is unlikely because . . .
This is doubtful.
There may be another explanation for this fact.
  For example, . . .
These views are open to doubt.
Serious doubts can be raised against this.
However, . . .
This is nonsense.
```

◆ **TASK 14.** With a partner, choose one of the following topic statements, or choose a topic of your own. One of you will argue in favor of the topic; the other will argue against it. When you have finished your discussion, write a paragraph summarizing the arguments for and against the topic. Begin by stating the opposing views. Then present arguments to support your position. Try to use some of the language of refutation suggested above.

1. Many teenagers have been injured or killed as a result of drunk driving. Clearly, the legal drinking age needs to be raised.
2. The minimum TOEFL score required of foreign students for university admissions should be raised, thereby eliminating students who are not likely to succeed in their work.
3. Using surrogate mothers to produce babies for childless couples is one of the most exciting new by-products of modern scientific research.
4. More emphasis must be placed on the sciences and less on the arts and humanities in elementary and secondary schools.

SUMMARY TASK

◆ Choose one of the following topics, and write an argument for or against it.

1. Write an argument in favor or against a mandatory seat belt law. You might want to refer to Task 7 and 11 on pages 53 and 56.
2. Write an argument in favor of or against using English as the official international language.

Remember to start by thinking of as many statements in favor of your topic as possible. Then decide which ones are relevant and which ones are not. Eliminate the irrelevant ones. Be sure you have sufficient support for your argument. Then organize your reasons.

After you have written your arguments, decide what organizational signals you need to make your paragraph clearer.

When you have finished, exchange papers with a partner. Look at your partner's paper and decide:

1. What is the main argument?
2. How many reasons does the writer have?
3. Are the reasons relevant to the topic?
4. Are there enough reasons and supporting statements to convince you of the writer's point of view?
5. Are there organizational signals to help you understand the argument better?
6. Is there a concluding statement or paragraph?

Return your partner's paper and discuss your ideas about it. When you and your partner have finished discussing each other's papers, rewrite your paper with your partner's suggestions in mind.

Writing about Problems and Solutions

GETTING STARTED

Often it is necessary to examine problems and find the best solutions for them. The first step in this kind of writing is to state the problem clearly. Sometimes you must say what will happen if the problem is not solved, that is, what the consequences will be.

◆ Look at the illustration of the car. What is wrong with the car? What are the possible consequences of each problem? Compare your answers with those of another student.

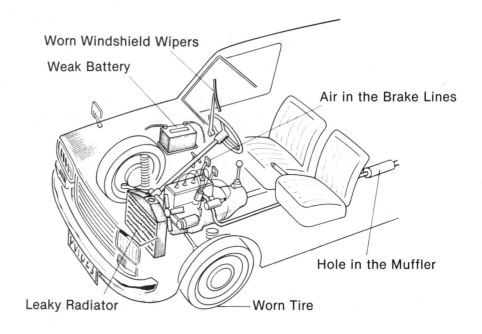

Worn Windshield Wipers

Weak Battery

Air in the Brake Lines

Hole in the Muffler

Leaky Radiator

Worn Tire

In this final chapter, you will practice describing problems, offering solutions, and predicting consequences.

IDENTIFYING PROBLEMS

◆ **TASK 1.**   Here is the beginning of a list of problems that face many urban cities today:

- Severe traffic jams
- Homeless people
- High rents

Look at a local newspaper and identify other problems which face the city you now live in.

Useful Language for Describing Problems

Many problems can be described in terms of *too much* or *too little* of something. The following lists suggest other expressions which can be used to identify a problem. Notice that the expressions in the first column are used only with countable nouns (such as *cars*). The expressions in the second column are used with uncountable nouns (such as *traffic*). The expressions in the third column can be used with both countable and uncountable nouns.

Expressions with Countable Nouns	**Expressions with Uncountable Nouns**	**Expressions with all Nouns**
too many	too much	an excess of
too few	too little	not enough
an excessive number of	an excessive amount of	inadequate, insufficient
		a shortage of
		a lack of

◆ **TASK 2.**   What are some problems that confront students? Make a list of those problems. Which ones do you face? Discuss your list with another student. Try to use some of the language for describing problems suggested above.

DESCRIBING CONSEQUENCES

◆ **TASK 3.**   Study the information on the chart. Then look at the diet of a manual worker in a tropical country. What is wrong with it? State the problem and describe the possible consequences of living on such a diet.

Vitamins and Protein	Principal Vitamin/ Protein Sources	Principal Effect of Vitamin/ Protein Deficiencies
vitamin A	milk, butter, eggs, green and yellow vegetables	blindness
vitamin B	rice, meat, eggs	disorders of the nervous system
vitamin C	fruit, vegetables	skin diseases
vitamin D	sunlight, fish, liver, eggs	bone disease
protein	meat, fish, eggs, milk, beans	malnutrition

Minimum Levels for Health	
carbohydrates	150 grams
protein	56 grams

Average Daily Intake of an Adult Male Manual Worker in a Tropical Country

- rice, bread (carbohydrates)   400 grams
- oils, fats (carbohydrates)   50 grams
- meat   25 grams
- fresh fruit and vegetables   10 grams
- beans   25 grams
- milk and dairy products   0
- fish   0

Useful Language for Describing Consequences

If-sentences are useful to predict the consequences of actions. For example, in discussing the improper diet of the worker in Task 3, you might say:

> He doesn't consume enough dairy products. *If* he *doesn't increase* his intake of vitamin A, he *may become* blind.

Note that the present tense is used for the action, and the future tense for the consequence when you are discussing real possibilities or proposals.

When describing consequences, you can also use expressions such as *will certainly, may, could,* or *might not* to show how certain you are of the results. Look at page 80 in the reference section for additional expressions and explanations.

◆ **TASK 4.** Look at this problem situation.

Country Y is a small, land-locked, Central Asian state. In the past, its economy was based on the export of rice, animal by-products, and the money sent home by those who found work in neighboring countries. Now tourism is expanding rapidly as the magnificent mountains and the unique temples of that country, although unfortunately in very poor condition, become better known.

Although the people are cheerful and hard-working, country Y has many problems. Infant mortality is 50%. In spite of this, the population is increasing rapidly. Farming techniques are very old-fashioned and food now has to be imported. Much of the land is badly-eroded hillside and semi-desert. This is due partly to the destruction of forests to provide wood for heat and cooking fires. Illiteracy is above 90%. Country Y is a non-aligned state but has a dispute with her much bigger southern neighbor over irrigation rights of the river which forms the frontier between the two countries.

A. The main items in country Y's five-year plan are given in the following chart. Predict the consequences of each proposal. Then write your predictions, using some of the language discussed in this chapter for describing consequences. The first one is done for you.

Ministry	Plan	Consequences
Education	Establish a university	*Will bring little benefit to the country*
Tourism	Reconstruct the temples	
Power	Construct a dam across the river to generate electricity	
Health	Sterilize all parents with more than three children	
Agriculture	Extend the river irrigation scheme	
Defense	Buy fighter aircraft	

B. Can you think of alternatives to this five-year plan, alternatives which you consider to have more favorable consequences? Write your suggestions and discuss them with another student. For example, you might propose the following: *Building more elementary schools will certainly help reduce the extraordinarily high rate of illiteracy.*

PRESENTING AND COMPARING SOLUTIONS

Usually several solutions can be suggested to any problem. One way of talking about alternatives is to use another type of *if*-sentence. In these sentences, the past tense describes the action, and *would, might,* or *could* describe the consequences. This type of conditional sentence describes proposals which are still under discussion and have not yet been agreed to.

Compare the two statements in the following example. The first suggests the consequences of real proposals or possibilities; the second describes hypothetical, or unrealized proposals.

> *If* the government *establishes* a university, and this is indeed the plan, it *will bring* little benefit to the country. However, *if* they *built* more elementary schools, which is unfortunately not being considered as part of the plan, illiteracy *would be reduced.*

After each alternative solution has been stated, it must be examined and the best one chosen. This is usually done by comparing and contrasting them according to effectiveness, benefits, cost, undesirable consequences, etc.

◆ **TASK 5.**   Study this problem and the proposed solutions.

Hospitals in country T are very short of blood. People will not willingly give blood because they feel it will weaken them. In addition, there is a strong caste system and people who give blood are afraid it will go to someone of lower caste. Furthermore, about 10% of the population belong to a religion which believes that giving blood is wrong. In these circumstances, how can the hospitals in country T build up a blood bank?

Problem
Insufficient blood.

Solution 1	Solution 2	Solution 3	Solution 4
Set up a voluntary blood donation service. Educate people so that they will willingly give blood.	Buy blood. Pay a high price for each 500 c.c. of blood provided.	Refuse to admit patients to hospitals unless their families agree to provide blood.	Pass a law so that every adult must give blood once a year.

A. Write the solutions from the chart. Add a solution of your own. Then predict the consequences of adopting each of these solutions.

Solution	Consequences
1	
2	
3	
4	
Own	

B. Complete this table, listing the good and bad points of each solution.

Solution	Good points	Bad points
1	free	will take a long time
2		
3		
4		
Own		

C. Using the completed tables and the predictions you made, write a short comparison and contrast of the proposed solutions. Try to use some of the language presented in this chapter. If necessary, you can also turn to Chapter 4 for a review of comparing and contrasting.

MAKING RECOMMENDATIONS

> The final step in writing about problems and solutions is making recommendations. To summarize, a paragraph or essay of this kind should:
>
> 1. State the problem
> 2. Compare and contrast solutions
> 3. Recommend the best solution

In making recommendations, you need to decide how forcefully you want to make them. The language you choose to express these recommendations can range from the most urgent—*it is imperative that ...* —to a mere suggestion—*it might be advisable*. For additional language and explanations turn to page 80 in the reference section.

Regardless of the strength of your recommendation, it has to be supported by reasons which will convince your reader.

◆ **TASK 6.** Look at the map of the city and its surroundings. Read about the problems the city is facing.

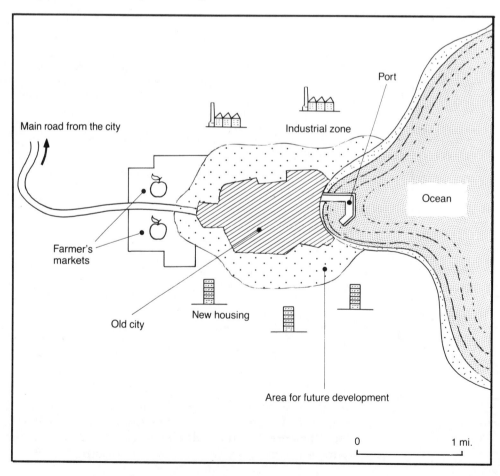

In the past, this capital city was a fishing port and a center for pearl diving. However, the country as a whole has developed rapidly over the past 20 years and, as a result, the city has expanded. Heavy industry has been developed to the north of the city, well removed from the new housing projects in the south where many of the workers live. The port, too, has grown in size because trade has increased.

Farmer's markets have grown up on the west side of the city to meet the growing demand for fresh vegetables and fruit. The old center of the city remains almost unchanged. The streets are narrow and winding. The houses are old and some are in poor condition, but they are typical of the old style of architecture in the country. Unfortunately, all the traffic must pass through the old center. Therefore, there are constant traffic jams.

A. Study the possible solutions to the city's traffic problems. Add three more solutions of your own.

Problem
Traffic jams in the city center.

Solution 1	**Solution 2**	**Solution 3**
Build a subway beneath the old city.	Build a bridge over the old city to link the industrial area with the new housing.	Provide a ferry boat service for workers from the south to the industrial area in the north.

Solution 4	**Solution 5**	**Solution 6**
build a ring road round the city centre.	build better roads through the city centre.	regulate car access limit / provide better public transport.

B. Write a short summary of the city's traffic problems. Start with a paragraph describing the problem. Use the information in the map and the descriptive paragraphs. Then consider all the solutions, both those given in the chart and those you have added. Predict the consequences of adopting each solution. Finally, make recommendations.

◆ **TASK 7.** Look at this map. It shows four possible sites for a cement factory. Using the information in the map, recommend the best location. List as many reasons as you can to support your recommendation. Then compare your recommendation with those of the other members of your class. Decide which ones are the most convincing.

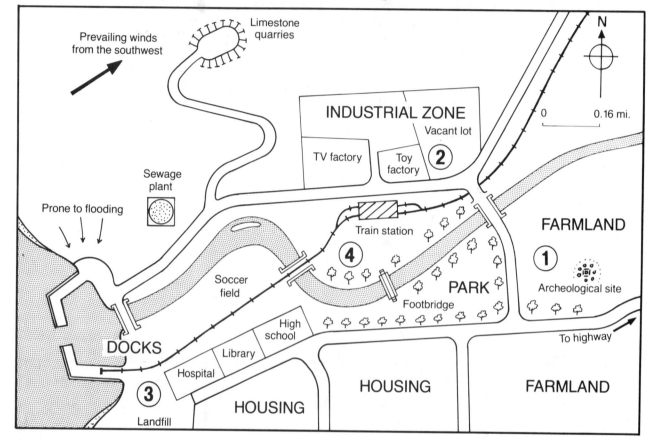

◆ **TASK 8.** Look at the map again. Recommend the best location for the following development projects, and give reasons for your recommendations. Exchange your recommendations with another student who will decide whether or not they are convincing. If they are not convincing, your classmate must offer reasons for rejecting them and suggest alternatives.

1. A new elementary school
2. A new restaurant
3. A new shopping center

CONCLUDING PARAGRAPHS

A concluding paragraph allows you to summarize, and therefore repeat, the main points in your writing. It reminds your reader of the most important points and helps you get your message across.

◆ **TASK 9.** Read the following description of ways of solving the energy crisis. List the main points. Compare your list with the one on page 81 of the reference section.

Nuclear power has often been presented as the only means of "saving" our standard of living when the fossil fuels like oil, coal, and gas run out. It is attractive in that we have already developed the technology to exploit the energy stored in the atom. In addition, small amounts of fuel release enormous amounts of energy.

However, the problems of nuclear power have become increasingly clear in the last decade. These range from the threat of pollution to the danger of an accidental explosion, and these make nuclear power a less desirable solution to the energy crisis. Furthermore, to completely replace fossil fuels by nuclear power would require the construction of about fifty times the present number of nuclear power stations by the end of the century, which is beyond our resources.

The role of alternative energy sources, such as solar energy, wave power, and wind power, has been researched in many countries. Studies in the U.S.A. have suggested that solar energy could provide 20% of U.S. heating and cooling requirements by the end of the century. The same research indicates that in several countries, including Britain, wind power might be of value. Wave power could also be an important source of electrical energy.

Of these sources, solar energy in the northern hemisphere is most available where it is least needed—in the middle of the day and in summer. Moreover, existing methods of energy transfer for solar power are relatively inefficient. If long-term storage could be devised so that energy available in peak periods of supply could be stored for use in peak periods of demand, much greater use could be made of solar power. In contrast, wave and wind power availability match the curve of energy demand, that is, the winds are strongest and the tides are highest during the winter. For the present, wind power is by far the cheapest of these alternative sources. It requires, however, aerogenerators, as big as electricity pylons, located along coastlines, where they could be very ugly.

Using energy from the waves is still in its experimental stages. In the long run, it is likely to be more expensive than wind power, but may still be cheaper than nuclear power.

Some people argue that the huge coal reserves in some countries make the search for new sources of energy less urgent. But this is not facing the facts. They forget that new demands will almost certainly be made on our coal reserves as a source of plastics. Coal is much too valuable to burn.

◆ **TASK 10.** Write a concluding paragraph to the passage on energy in Task 9. Use your list of main points to help you summarize the discussion. Then read the paragraph on page 81 of the reference section for comparison.

SUMMARY TASK

◆ Choose a problem from the suggestions below, or choose one of your own. Describe the problem and the possible consequences if the problem is not solved. Discuss solutions and make recommendations.

- Problems faced by foreign students
- Unequal distribution of wealth in the world
- The increase in teen-age suicides
- The problem of drunk driving
- Experiments in genetic engineering
- Shyness

In this final writing, take the opportunity to review the aspects of writing presented in this book. Here is a list to help you get started.

1. List ideas before beginning to write.
2. Select information with your reader in mind.
3. Supply supporting details.
4. Organize your information.
5. Use language to link statements within and between paragraphs.
6. Divide paragraphs clearly.
7. Describe, explain, define, or argue convincingly.
8. Clearly state your main ideas.
9. Include a concluding statement.
10. Reread and revise your writing.

Reference Section

1 Preparing to Write

GETTING STARTED (page 1) Description of Bruce Springsteen

Compare this description of Bruce Springsteen with the one you wrote.

> Bruce Springsteen was born on September 23, 1949, in New Jersey. His nickname is "The Boss." He is of Dutch descent. His parents live in California. He still lives in New Jersey. He is a musician, a composer, and a bandleader. He is considered the hardest-working rock 'n' roller of them all. In his free time, he works out, goes driving, and plays music. He is 5 feet 10 inches tall. He has a powerful, raspy voice. He is known all over the world.

How is this description similar to or different from yours? List the similarities or differences. Then look at this edited version of the same description.

> Bruce Springsteen, whose nickname is "The Boss," is considered the hardest-working rock 'n' roller of them all. Although he is only 5 feet 10 inches tall, he has a powerful, raspy voice which is recognized all over the world. Not only is he a musician, but he is also a composer and a bandleader. In his free time, he plays music, works out, and goes driving. Of Dutch descent, Springsteen was born on September 23, 1949, in New Jersey, where he still lives, although his parents now live in California.

With your partner, examine what changes the editor made and how these changes improved the description. For example, compare the number of sentences in each version. How have the sentences been ordered? Which information is more important? How do you know?

In the first draft of the description, each fact about Springsteen appeared in a separate sentence. As a result, each fact has equal importance. In the edited version, some facts have been combined. Also, some facts have been given more importance than others. How do we know that some facts are more important than others? Facts that are in main clauses are more important than facts that are in subordinate clauses or in phrases. What are main clauses, subordinate clauses, and phrases? You will learn what these are in the chapters that follow.

Did you notice that the order of information was also changed? The information about Springsteen's current life came first. Information about his background came later.

This exercise was just to get your feet wet, to give you an idea of the process of getting ideas on paper, putting them together in sentences, and arranging these ideas in sentences and paragraphs. All this determines the effect your writing will have on the reader. Let's return now to Unit One on page 1 and get started on the first stages of writing.

TASK 1   (page 2) Description of a City

Here is a list of possible points you might cover in a description of a city:

1. location
2. population
3. climate
4. history
5. industry and commerce
6. places of interest
7. shopping areas
8. entertainment
9. types of accommodations
10. local government
11. architecture
12. educational facilities
13. sports facilities
14. transportation
15. famous people

TASK 8   (page 6) Additional Practice with Relative Clauses

A. Define the words in column *A* using the information from the other columns. For example, *A laboratory is a place where experiments can be made.*

A	B	C
1. a laboratory		has six legs and no backbone
2. a historian		studies language
3. a farm	a person	is concerned with matter and energy
4. an insect	a place	
5. a linguist	an animal	studies the past
6. a library	a science	experiments can be made
7. a spokesperson		crops are grown or animals kept
8. physics		books are kept for borrowing
		speaks for a group

B. Write your own definition of these terms. Compare your definitions with those of another student, then with those in a dictionary.

1. a university
2. a democracy
3. geography
4. a psychologist
5. oxygen
6. socialism
7. a student
8. a teacher
9. a profession
10. cancer

C. Rewrite this paragraph. Use relative clauses to include the italicized information in parentheses. If the information is simply descriptive, separate the clauses from the main clause with commas. For example, the first sentence of your paragraph will be: *The Olympic Games are an international athletic competition which takes place every four years.*

The Olympic Games are an international athletic competition. (*This international competition takes place every four years.*) The name comes from the part of Greece called Olympia. (*The Games were first held in Olympia over 2,000 years ago.*) Competitors competed not just in athletics, but also in music, poetry, and other arts. (*Competitors came from all parts of Greece.*) The modern Olympics concentrate mainly on athletics. (*The modern Olympics were started in 1896.*) The Games open with a ceremony. (*The ceremony is based on the original Greek one.*) The Olympic torch is carried by runners. (*Runners bring the flame from Olympia.*) At the end of the ceremony, hundreds of doves are released. (*Doves are a symbol of peace.*)

 # Describing, Comparing, and Contrasting

TASK 1 (page 26) Describing Objects

It's a red bag that looks like a small suitcase. It's about 12 inches by 16 inches. It's got two handles and a zipper on top and two zippered side pockets. The top is made of smooth plastic and the sides are textured plastic. Inside, there's a binder, and a biology and an accounting textbook.

TASK 2 (page 26) Describing Objects

> Sturdy, spacious red bookbag to carry all your textbooks and school supplies and even your lunch. Hardly used, must sell, good price.

TASK 5 (page 27) Describing Similarities and Differences

1. in different ways (D); whereas (D); while (D)
2. is like (S); Both (S); is very different from (D); neither . . . nor (S)
3. although (D); Unlike (D)
4. whereas (D); are not as . . . as (D); by contrast (D); as well as (S)

TASK 6 (page 28) Comparing Similarities and Differences

1. more effectively; better; more easily than; faster than; more willing
2. more familiar than; more specialized; faster; more maneuverable

 Describing Processes, Developments, and Graphs

GETTING STARTED (page 32) How to Make a Paper Airplane

a. Use a sheet of 8 1/2 × 11 inch paper and fold the paper in half lengthwise.
b. Open the paper and fold one corner down toward the center crease.
c. Fold the other corner down in the same way.
d. Fold each side toward the center.
e. Turn the paper over.
f. With the paper turned over, fold one side over along the left-hand dotted line shown in drawing 7.
g. With the paper turned over, fold the other side over along the right-hand dotted line in drawing 7.
h. Tape the body of the plane together.

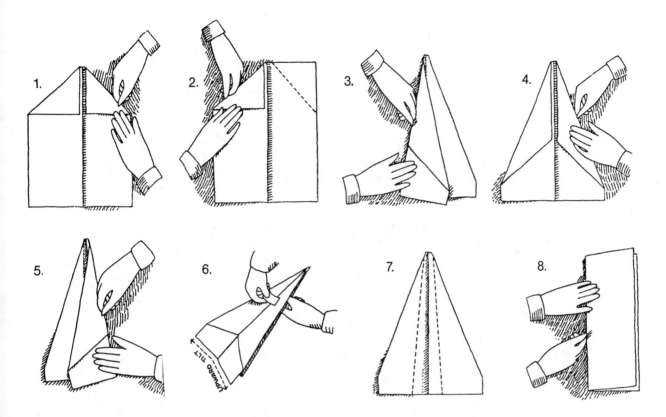

1.   2.   3.   4.

5.   6.   7.   8.

TASK 2 (page 34) The Passive Voice

In active sentences, the subject performs the action of the verb. For example:

The German emperor visited the city.
      (subject)

Here, the subject, *the German emperor,* did the visiting.

In passive sentences, the subject does not perform the action of the verb. For example:

In 1916, the Germans were defeated by the British.
        (subject)

Here, the subject, *the Germans,* did not do the defeating; the British did. In passive sentences, the agent (or person doing the action) is expressed in a phrase beginning with *by.* When the agent is not important or is unknown, it simply is not expressed at all. For example:

In 1916, the Germans were defeated.

Subject + a form of the verb *be* + past participle + by + agent
                      of the verb   (optional)

The Germans + were   + defeated   + (by the British)

A. Use the passive voice to complete the description of each of the steps in the process of making bread.

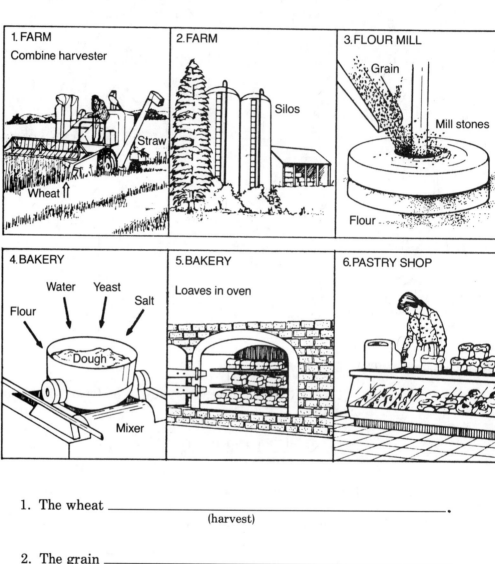

1. The wheat _____.
   (harvest)

2. The grain _____.
   (store)

3. The grain _____ into flour.
   (make)

4. The flour _____ with other ingredients.
   (mix)

5. The mixture _____ into loaves.
   (bake)

6. The loaves _____ in retail stores.
   (sell)

B. Describe a process with which you are familiar, such as using a machine, making food, playing an instrument. Use the passive voice whenever possible. Read your description to your classmates.

TASK 6 (page 39) Useful Language to Describe Change

Look at the period 1920–1930 in the graph on page 38. You can describe this part of the graph in two ways:

- By using a verb of change. For example: Cigarette smoking *rose.*
- By using a related noun. For example: There was *a rise* in cigarette smoking.

You can also add an adverb or adjective to describe the rate of change. For example:

- Cigarette smoking rose *gradually.*
- There was a *gradual* rise in cigarette smoking.

Here is a table of verbs and related nouns often used in describing graphs.

Direction	Verbs of change	Nouns of change
UP	rise increase climb go up	rise increase — —
DOWN	fall decline decrease dip drop go down	fall decline decrease dip drop —
LEVEL	level out not change remain steady	leveling out no change —

Study the adjectives used to describe the change in the graph below:

gradual	sharp	rapid	slight
slight	steep	abrupt	slow

All of these adjectives, except *steep,* have adverbial forms:

gradually	sharply	rapidly	slightly
slightly		abruptly	slowly

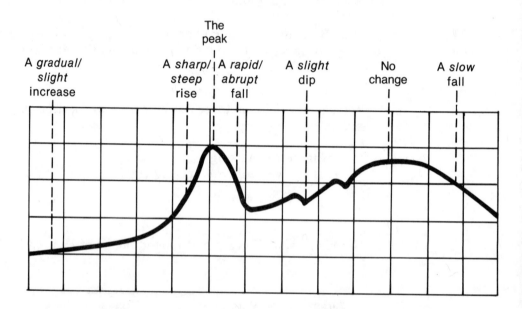

A. Rewrite each of these sentences using a noun to describe change. The first one is done for you.

1. Between 1920 and 1930 cigarette smoking increased gradually.

   Between 1920 and 1930 there was a gradual increase in cigarette smoking.

2. Between 1945 and 1950 cigarette smoking fell sharply.

3. Between 1968 and 1972 cigarette consumption did not change.

4. Between 1956 and 1958 cigarette smoking dipped slightly.

B. Describe the graph on page 38 for these periods, using either a verb or noun of change.

1. 1940–1945	3. 1961–1964
2. 1972–1980	4. 1951–1956

Compare your answers with those of other students.

TASK 7 (page 39) Possible Reasons for Change in Cigarette Smoking Patterns

1920s Men changed from pipes to cigarettes.
       Women started to smoke.
1930s Many people were without work.
1939   The Second World War began.
1945   The War ended.
       Only essential items were imported.
1951   Import bans were lifted.
1957   The tax on tobacco was increased.
1962   Tobacco tax was again increased.
1960s The war in Vietnam became more serious.
1968   An anti-smoking campaign started.
1970s Artificial tobacco was introduced.
       The link between cancer and smoking
       became increasingly clear.

6 Writing Explanations

GETTING STARTED (page 41) Why Does a Ball Bounce?

Balls bounce because they are made of rubber, which is an elastic material. Such materials try to regain their original shape when they are distorted. When a ball hits a hard surface, it is flattened. The elasticity of the rubber then causes it to regain its original shape.

7 Writing Arguments

TASK 12 (page 57) Refuting an Argument

Members of the Flat Earth Society claim that the Earth is flat. They say that we would all fall off if it were round. This is nonsense. We know that the world is round because if we travel far enough in any direction, we will eventually arrive back where we started. We do not fall off because we are held to the Earth by gravity.

Writing about Problems and Solutions

TASK 3 (page 62) Useful Language for Describing Consequences

The chart below lists some expressions that are used to show how certain you are of the consequences described. The greater number of stars (*) on the chart, the greater the degree of certainty.

Degree of certainty	Positive	Negative
****	will certainly	will not impossible that
***	likely that probable that probably	unlikely that improbable that
**	may, might possible that possibly	may not might not
*	could	

TASK 6 (page 66) Making Recommendations

Study these verbs and expressions used to make recommendations in writing.

URGENT RECOMMENDATIONS

Using modal verbs	Using *be* + adjective + *that*
must have to need to	be imperative that be essential that be important that

GENERAL RECOMMENDATIONS

Using modal verbs	Using noun + *be* + *that*	Using *be* + adjective + *to*	Using verbs
should	(my) advice is that suggestion is that recommendation is that finding is that	be advisable to	advise (someone) to suggest (that) recommend (that)

TASK 9 (page 69) Solving the Energy Crisis: Main Points

1. nuclear power not the complete solution; possibly dangerous; too expensive
2. alternative energy sources should be considered
3. solar energy: inefficient storage
   wind: cheap but unsightly
   waves: still experimental
4. coal reserves large but too valuable

TASK 10 (page 69) Solving Energy Crisis: Concluding Paragraph

We have shown that nuclear power is not the complete answer to the energy problem. There are problems of safety and cost. Alternative sources such as sun, wave and wind power have to be considered but, as we have seen, none is ideal. Solar power cannot be stored easily. Wind power is cheap but requires many ugly aerogenerators. Wave power is still in the experimental stages. Coal reserves are huge but, as a valuable source of raw material for plastics, should not be wasted. A satisfactory solution to the energy problem is still to be found.

We wish to thank the following for providing us with photographs:

Page 1, courtesy of Bruce Springsteen. **Page 2,** Citibank, Citicorp. **Page 18,** United Airlines photo.

We wish to thank the following artists:

Robin Jacques, G. J. Galsworthy, Oxford illustrators, Joseph DePinho, and Steven Shindler. Special thanks to H. J. L. Mantell A.R.I.B.A. for his work on the illustrations.

We wish to thank the following for permission to reproduce copyright material:

Page 60, Longman Group Ltd. for adapted diagram from *Mainline Skills A,* 1975. **Page 75,** Viking Penguin Inc. for illustration from *The Paper Airplaine Book,* by Seymour Simon, 1986.

Notes

Notes

Notes

Notes

Notes

Notes